The Baby Blues

Also by Drew Hayden Taylor

PLAYS

alterNatives*
The Baby Blues*
The Berlin Blues*
The Bootlegger Blues
The Boy in the Treehouse / Girl Who Loved Her Horses*
The Buz'Gem Blues*
Dead White Writer on the Floor*
400 Kilometres*
God and the Indian*
In a World Created by a Drunken God*
Only Drunks and Children Tell the Truth*
Someday
Toronto at Dreamer's Rock / Education Is Our Right

FICTION

Fearless Warriors*
Motorcycles and Sweetgrass
The Night Wanderer

NON-FICTION

Me Funny
Me Sexy
NEWS: Postcards from the Four Directions*

* *Available from Talonbooks*

The Baby Blues

Drew Hayden Taylor

TALONBOOKS

Talonbooks
278 East First Avenue, Vancouver, British Columbia, Canada V5T 1A6
www.talonbooks.com

Seventh printing: April 2014

Typeset in New Baskerville
Printed and bound in Canada on 100% post-consumer recycled paper

Cover design by Adam Swica

Talonbooks gratefully acknowledges the financial support of the Canada Council for the Arts, the Government of Canada through the Canada Book Fund, and the Province of British Columbia through the British Columbia Arts Council and the Book Publishing Tax Credit.

Rights to produce *The Baby Blues*, in whole or in part, in any medium by any group, amateur or professional, are retained by the author. Interested persons are requested to contact his agent: Janine Cheeseman, Aurora Artists Agency, 19 Wroxeter Avenue, Toronto, Ontario M4K 1J5; tel.: (416) 463-4634; fax: (416) 463-4889; email: aurora.artists@sympatico.ca

Library and Archives Canada Cataloguing in Publication

Taylor, Drew Hayden, 1962–
  The baby blues

  A play.
  ISBN 0-88922-406-4

  I. Title.
PS8589.A885B32 1999   C812'.54   C99-910221-4
PR9199.3.T35B32 1999

*The journey to seeing **The Baby Blues** produced, then published, was a long one – a journey that involved many special people who offered their talents, in many different ways, towards the final product you now hold in your hands. I would like to send an aboriginal "much thanks" to the following: Elizabeth Theobald, Randy Reinholz, David Ferry, Brian Richmond, Lynda Hill, Larry Lewis (where it all began), Pennsylvania Centre Stage, Mark Taper Forum, Native Voices, Arbor Theatre, and Native Earth Performing Arts. If I'm doing anyone the disservice of leaving them out, please forgive me. Those who are not here physically in ink are here in spirit.*

Needless to say, ch'meegwetch to all the fine and talented people who have appeared or worked on my humble little play over the years. See you at the next great adventure! The first coffee's on me.

Foreword

Chapter One, Verse One:

The Early Years. Tuesday, to be specific. Then again, it might have been Wednesday. No, it was definitely Tuesday.

Welcome to the world of *The Baby Blues*, a trip to the funny bone of my (and almost a million others') aboriginal universe.

The Baby Blues is part of The Blues Quartet, a series of four plays all totally independent from one another. The first installment in the series is *The Bootlegger Blues*. The next to make its way onto the stage will be *The Buz'Gem Blues*. The fourth ... who knows? All four are designed as a way of applauding the humour and merriment that exist in today's Native community. After many decades of seeing the media highlight the image of the "tragic" or "stoic" Indian, I felt Native people, and consequently non-Native people, were being given a raw deal. I know far more laughing First Nations people than depressed ones. I felt this disproportionate representation had to be addressed.

Thus, *The Blues Quartet*, a series of plays that have their roots in the belly laughs of the communities. And in our history.

At the centre of many First Nations mythologies is a character know simply as the Trickster. Though in some areas of this continent known by its indigenous inhabitants as Turtle Island, the Trickster can and does go by many names: Glooscap, Raven, Coyote, Old Man, Weesageechak, and, in my Ojibway nation, Nanabush. This wondrous character is a glorious celebration of the mischievous, the joke, the play, and I guess in the end, the art of the storyteller.

Welcome to my little play. I try to keep true to that Trickster spirit, for I wrote what some have called a Native version of a British sex farce as a celebration of the aboriginal sense of humour. Anybody who knows the Native community will hopefully recognize some of the characters.

One thing I am sure of is that for true comedy to work properly, it has to be universal. While the details and specifics of this play are pure Native Indian, I don't think there's a person reading this book or seeing the play, regardless of their heritage, who won't relate to the people they see onstage – whether it be a mother dealing with a rebellious daughter, a good-looking young man on the hustle, or a man who refuses to acknowledge the passing years.

But then again, maybe these things don't happen in your life. If so, consider yourself very lucky.

– Drew Hayden Taylor

The Baby Blues premiered at the Arbor Theatre in Peterborough, Ontario, on February 21, 1995, with the following cast and crew:

NOBLE .... Buffalo Child
JENNY .... Michelle Goodeve
AMOS .... Vince Manitowabi
PASHIK .... Lura Merritt
SKUNK .... Levi Aguonie
SUMMER .... Thea Gill

Directed by Brian Richmond
Set and costume design by Yvonne Sauriol
Lighting design by Lynne Hyde
Stage management by Detlev Fuellbeck

Characters

NOBLE	An aging fancy dancer who refuses to grow up, thirty-eight years old
JENNY	An independent and strong woman who can handle the world, thirty-seven years old
AMOS	A Mohawk elder who travels the powwow trail dispensing food and wisdom, sixty years old
PASHIK	Jenny's daughter, a teenager who wants to see the world, no matter what her mother says, seventeen years old
SKUNK	A young and rakish fancy dancer, everything Noble once was, twenty years old
SUMMER	A non-Native woman who is travelling the powwow trail seeking knowledge, twenty-five years old

Setting

A typical powwow venue, including a campground and an area with food stands. Set on a lazy summer day on a reserve somewhere in Central Ontario.

ACT ONE

Scene One

*The lights come up on a campground down by a lake.
It is a beautiful, hot summer day and the place looks
deserted except for the sounds of kids laughing and
splashing in the water. NOBLE enters laden with a big,
awkward, ancient-looking canvas tent. Sunglasses on
his face hide his hungover and bloodshot eyes from the
world. He is singing Rod Stewart's "Do You Think I'm
Sexy?" or something similar through his pain. After
dropping his tent, he spots, off in the distance, a
familiar face he waves to, then another, and then he
spots somebody he is trying to avoid. He pulls his
baseball cap down and ducks behind a bush. He
quickly scurries offstage.*

*A young woman enters looking vaguely hippie/new age-
ish. She wears gobs and gobs of turquoise and beaded
jewellery and other Native adornments. She is obviously
in love with her surroundings. She clasps a flower to
her chest. In her other hand she holds a small tape
recorder that she turns on.*

SUMMER: Testing, testing. This is Summer and I'm
here at an actual, real-life powwow! Oh, how
beautiful, simply so beautiful. Just smell that
woodsmoke, the bacon frying – what a pity I don't
eat meat. Oh, listen to the children of nature
playing, being one with the lake. Oh, it is bliss,

sheer bliss. The harmony I feel in this place. Here I am, surrounded by trees, flowers, grass, squirrels and Native people. Tree to tree, First Nations. Aboriginal people in their natural environment. Indigena everywhere! Oh, I hope I have the honesty and spirit to open myself up to these people and show them my purity of heart so they will accept me into their fold. These people have so much to teach us. But ... but ... I must not appear too eager. That's what wannabees do, and Creator forbid, I certainly am not one of them. I merely want to share experiences with them, and be taught their teachings.

At this point, SKUNK enters wearing a towel. He sizes her up for a moment before approaching. SUMMER is oblivious to him until he is standing right beside her.

SUMMER: But how to start? I must not appear too forceful or pushy. Maybe I should just walk through the campsites. Yes, and maybe someone will spot my beaded earrings, notice my thirst for knowledge, and ask if I want to share a meal, or maybe participate in a sunrise ceremony or something ...

SKUNK: I wouldn't count on it.

SUMMER, turning off the recorder, turns to SKUNK.

SUMMER: Pardon?

SKUNK: Sun's been up a couple hours. No point in having a sunrise ceremony if the sun's up already. Be like saying grace after the meal.

SUMMER: Of course, how silly of me. I'm kinda new at this.

SKUNK: I figured.

SUMMER: Hi, my name is Summer. I am here in search of knowledge.

SKUNK: First-year anthropology or sociology student?

SUMMER: Anthropology. How did you know?

SKUNK: We Natives have a sixth sense about these things. Summer's an unusual name.

SUMMER: I like it much better than my Christian name – Agnes. Oh, I'm sorry, I didn't offend you by using the word "Christian," did I? I'm really sorry.

SKUNK: No, that's okay, no problem, some of my best friends are Christians. So what are you doing here?

SUMMER: I'm here for the powwow. I want to see the dancing, feel the power of the drum, breathe in the essence of being Native.

SKUNK: Uh-huh. You're not exactly Native yourself, are you?

SUMMER: No, I admit it, I was raised as a member of the oppressive white majority that is responsible for the unfortunate economic and social conditions your people live in. But really, deep, deep down inside, I'm a good person. Really I am! That's why I took this Native studies class. Don't blame me for what they have done. I want to atone for their sins.

SKUNK: Right. Well, okay, whatever turns your crank.

SUMMER: But wait, you didn't let me finish. I am also taking Native studies because, though I have not been skilled in the ways of the elders, I do consider myself a part of the great aboriginal collective.

SKUNK: You do?

SUMMER: For though I stand before you, Caucasian in appearance, I want you, as my Native brother, to know I, too, carry the blood of your ancestors in my veins.

SKUNK: Nooooo!

SUMMER: It's the truth. I only found out last year. In our family archives I found evidence that my great-great-grandmother, Donna Seymour – may her spirit walk with the Grandmothers – was one-quarter Native.

SKUNK: You're kidding!

SUMMER: No, but I haven't yet found out what particular Nation she belonged to – or I for that matter – but we are all brothers and sisters in the fight against the white oppressor.

SKUNK: If your great-great-grandmother was one-quarter that would make you ...

SUMMER: I am proud to say one-sixty-fourth. And proud of every aboriginal cell in my body. Can you see it in my features?

SKUNK: Ah yeah, yeah, right around your ... um, nostrils.

SUMMER: You see it, too! I keep telling people. The genes are too strong to be diluted.

SKUNK: Party on, Pocahontas.

SUMMER: Excuse me but, if you don't mind my asking, where are you going with the towel? A sweat lodge maybe?

SKUNK: A swim.

SUMMER: Oh.

SUMMER looks disappointed and SKUNK catches this. His attitude changes.

14

SKUNK: Ah yes ... I'm going for my ... morning purification ... cleansing swim, in the lake ... Mother Earth's lake ... the tears of Mother Earth.

SUMMER: Really?!

SKUNK: Yes, I do it every morning ... to greet our brother the sun. Right around that bend is a secluded bay where I ... reveal myself to the world, pay homage to the land, the water, and the sun. And wash. If you want, you can join me. If you're into that, I mean.

SUMMER: Oh yes, yes, I'd be honoured. Is it permitted?

SKUNK: I don't see why not, but I must warn you: in order to reveal yourself to the world, you have to be ... completely naked.

SUMMER: That's part of the ritual?

SKUNK: Oh, it wouldn't be the same ritual without it. Trust me. Is this an aboriginal face that would lie?

SUMMER: No, I guess not. We are at a powwow and ... *no.* I will not allow my middle-class inhibitions to infringe upon these sacred ceremonies. I will do it.

SKUNK: (*surprised*) You will? Oh, good, I mean, well, better get a towel.

SUMMER: I have one in my car with all my other stuff. Just a moment.

SUMMER runs offstage. SKUNK smiles to himself and does a little dance. Looking around, he removes his bathing suit quickly from underneath his towel. He throws it into the bushes as SUMMER rushes back.

SUMMER: Okay, got my towel.

SKUNK puts his arm around SUMMER's shoulders as they walk offstage.

15

SKUNK: Great, now you'll have to do everything I say … By the way, my name is Skunk.

SUMMER: Is that your clan?

SKUNK: Whatever.

They exit the stage. There is a pause for a few seconds before NOBLE peeks to see if the coast is clear. It is and he appears, once again happy, carrying more camping gear and, in particular, a large radio blaring a song from the mid-seventies. He drops the gear and radio, singing along. His eye catches something and, after turning down the radio, walks over to the nearby bushes. He leans over to investigate and pulls out SKUNK's swimming trunks. He holds them up, somewhat surprised.

NOBLE: Must have been some party.

He stuffs them in his jean jacket, turns the radio up again, and exits. From the other direction, JENNY enters. She has a clipboard in her hand as she counts and marks the tents. She is followed by her daughter PASHIK. They are talking over each other's dialogue.

JENNY: Nope, nope, nope, nope, nope, I'm not listening. Nope, nope, nope …

PASHIK: Just listen to me. Come on, it's not that far. Really! Please, Mom?

JENNY: I can't hear you. What a beautiful day, look at that lake. Boy, the trees are tall today.

PASHIK turns off the radio.

PASHIK: Why won't you listen to me?

JENNY: Because I've got work to do. See, looks like we have a new arrival. Hasn't checked in yet. Great taste in music though.

16

PASHIK: Mother, this is your last chance. I will only ask you this one more time, and please keep in mind I am seventeen mature years old. One more year and I can do anything I wish, legally. If you let me go, I'll even make a deal with you.

JENNY: (*suspicious*) I'm not falling for that again. (*beat*) What kind of deal?

PASHIK: I'll stop telling people about that time you phoned up that Jesse Jim guy from *The Beachcombers* and asked him to marry you.

JENNY: Pashik! I told you to shut up about that. I was younger, stupider, more desperate.

PASHIK: So can I go? Come on, Mom. It's not that far.

JENNY: Hartford, Connecticut, isn't far! I've got to have a word with your geography teacher. We're in Canada, genius. Hartford is somewhere down in the States.

PASHIK: So what, we were a nomadic people once; I'm just trying to keep the tradition alive. And I figure any place you can get to by bus can't be all that far. So are you going to be daring and look at this rationally, or am I going to have to take this into my own hands?

JENNY: Go ahead, but remember, I have hands, too. And these hands are bigger, stronger, and more experienced than yours. Everything you've thrown at me I have overcome and won. You're still an amateur; I'm in the big leagues, kiddo.

PASHIK: We've all got to graduate sometime. And the old should retire.

JENNY: And what's so great about Connecticut, anyway?

PASHIK: Everybody I know is going to be there.

JENNY: I won't be.

PASHIK: An even better reason for me to go.

JENNY: I have one more year to get you through school. After you graduate, then the world is yours and they're welcome to you. Until then you're, as Mick used to sing, "Under My Thumb ..."

PASHIK: Mom ...

JENNY: It amazes me how kids can react to the word "yes" instantly but when you say "no," you have to keep saying it forever like they're deaf. No, no, no, no, no! Understand?

PASHIK: No.

JENNY: It must be genetic or something. Your father was like that the night I met him. One simple, stronger "no" back then and it would have saved me seventeen years of saying it to you.

PASHIK: Maybe that's why he left.

JENNY: He left because he was a schmuck. I've had cats with more loyalty than him – but don't bring him into it.

PASHIK: Why not? You do, except it's unconscious. You keep thinking that everything that happened to you is going to happen to me. Lightning doesn't always strike the same house twice. Some of us do plan for the future.

JENNY: Since when is going to Connecticut for some powwow planning for the future? Face it, kid, you're not going. Period. End of sentence. End of argument.

PASHIK: But ...

JENNY: No.

PASHIK: So it's war, then.

JENNY: When hasn't it been?

PASHIK: "All's fair ..."

JENNY: I remember you when you were just a little tiny baby. I used to have such a great time dressing you up in all those wonderful little dresses and treating you like the little girl you were. You would *goo* and *gah*, smile and laugh every time you saw me. You were better than a puppy. It was like having the sweetest, biggest most tanned Barbie doll anybody could ask for. Then you grew up. Why'd you have to grow up?!

PASHIK: I am my mother's daughter.

JENNY: And I hope your kids are the same. I should have taken it as a sign of things to come when you started teething while I breastfed you. Now leave me alone, I've got work to do. Go give somebody else an ulcer.

JENNY moves off scribbling on her clipboard. PASHIK watches her for a moment. JENNY notices and looks up.

JENNY: Pashik, it doesn't always have to be like this.

PASHIK: I'm going.

JENNY: Look, you're too young. I'm not going to let you take off to the other side of the border. You're only seventeen. God only knows what could happen to you. Mass murderers, rapists, rock stars. You can go when you're older.

PASHIK: Why do you always do that? Expect the worse.

JENNY: I'm a mother. And, more importantly, I'm your mother. I know you and I know the trouble you could get into. And I know the kind of people

19

out there waiting for young things like you. I know I'm probably blowing my chance of getting a present next Mother's Day, but it's the chance we mothers take. I'll just have to do without another T-shirt that says, Mothers Are God's Way of Preparing You for Hell.

JENNY pulls up her shirt to reveal her belly.

JENNY: See these stretch marks? They're sergeant stripes and you're still a private. That means you take orders from me. This place needs some more firewood. That's your assignment. About face, soldier.

PASHIK: But ...

JENNY: (*dangerously*) Now.

Grudgingly, PASHIK does as she's told.

JENNY: Now, march.

PASHIK marches offstage, fists clenched.

JENNY: They should have had me at Oka.

She goes back to her clipboard. NOBLE enters with the last of the camping equipment and turns the radio back up. He lets out an audible groan as he bends over to unroll his tent. JENNY wanders over to investigate.

JENNY: Excuse me.

NOBLE looks up and smiles his rakish smile.

NOBLE: Well, hello there, beautiful. If you're the welcome wagon, just grind me beneath your axles and I'll be in heaven.

JENNY: Slow down, there, cowboy; I've got a pounding migraine and I'm not in the mood. Now, first things first, your radio is a little loud. We'd appreciate it if you could keep it down.

Reluctantly, NOBLE turns off his radio.

NOBLE: A little music never hurt anybody.

JENNY: Hey, nobody likes vintage music more than me but the Bahá'i people over there were complaining. And it takes a hell of a lot to make a Bahá'i complain. So keep it down, for their sake. Now, I'm with the powwow committee. Just making sure people know where everything is. Toilets are over there (watch for spiders); the showers at the school are available from seven till nine in the morning (watch for mice); meals will be at the recreation centre across the road (watch out for cars); and ...

NOBLE: Lot of wildlife around here. I like that. The wilder the better ... know what I mean?

JENNY: No. Any other questions in a powwow-related field?

NOBLE: Yeah, which field is the powwow in? Ha!

NOBLE laughs at his own joke. JENNY just watches NOBLE until he realizes his best lines aren't working. He shifts gears.

NOBLE: Oh, come on, lady, lighten up. We're here to have fun. Tell you what, how about we go out later and ...

NOBLE watches PASHIK approaching with an armful of wood. She drops them with an angry thud at JENNY's feet, then storms away. NOBLE noticeably ogles her. This does not escape JENNY's attention.

JENNY: You were saying?

NOBLE: I forget. Who's the babe?

JENNY: You don't even pretend, do you?

NOBLE: (*his attention returns to JENNY*) Sorry. What?

JENNY: Why are you here?

NOBLE: What here? Here here?

JENNY: Why are you at this powwow?

NOBLE: To dance my little heart out and win big bucks.

JENNY: It's dancers like you that really piss me off.

NOBLE: Hey, I just got here. You can't pin anything on me.

JENNY: I've seen people like you at powwows from here to the Prairies. There are people on this trail who really love and respect it. They dance because they enjoy and honour what they're doing. It's not just some cheap excuse to take the summer off and make a few bucks.

NOBLE: Hey, I've been doin' it for almost twenty years now. You think it's fun sleeping on the ground for that long, in the rain, with mosquitoes, waking up after a party and not knowing where your underwear is? Don't you hate that? You're right, the dancing's gotta come from the soul but, hey, a guy's gotta have some fun.

JENNY: Yeah, yeah, I've heard it all before. Let me guess: "What happens outside the powwow grounds is my business." Isn't that the speech? Just stay out of my way.

NOBLE: So much for the welcome wagon. Only reserve I know with a "get the hell out of town" wagon.

JENNY: I've met too many of your type to waste time being nice. You spoil it for the rest of us.

JENNY exits, with one final glare. Perplexed, NOBLE watches her depart.

NOBLE: (*mockingly*) Somebody has an attitude.

He resumes putting his tent together.

NOBLE: Another powwow, another tent. It never seems to end. Boy, if I could count the number of times I've put this tent together, and the number of powwows I've been to in my life, I would have entirely too much time on my hands. But first, to find somebody to share this tent with.

NOBLE surveys the area and smiles at the familiarity. He pulls out his guitar and sits on the case as he starts to play "The Baby Blues."

I got in my truck and drove all the way here,
Hoping to find someone to call my sweet dear.
The road was dusty and the journey long,
Hoping for some fun, am I right or am I wrong.

Chorus
I've got the Baby Blues, you got it too.
Lookin' for love, every place I go,
When it comes to snaggin', I'm a pro.
I've got the Baby Blues right down to my toes,
I'm a hopeless romantic with nothing to lose.

The nights are long and the days are hot.
The beer may be cold but baby I'm not.
I've got fire for two, and a kiss for one,
Come on, honey, I can be a lot of fun.

Let's put our lips together and baby we'll hum,
Together we'll be louder than the biggest drum.
Person to person and Nation to Nation,
Before we're done, they'll call the fire station.

Repeat chorus

NOBLE is still fiddling with the last chords when
SKUNK enters, still wearing his towel. He goes to the
bush looking for his bathing suit. He becomes more and
more frustrated as he practically rips the bush apart.

SKUNK: Damn it! Where is that stupid thing?

This catches NOBLE's attention. He recognizes the bush
and pulls out the trunks from his pocket.

NOBLE: Yo, you in the skirt – looking for this?

SKUNK sees NOBLE holding up the trunks.

SKUNK: Hey, thanks, man. I was getting worried.
Those are the only trunks I got with me.

NOBLE: I found them in those bushes. That must
have been some fart.

NOBLE gives him the trunks and SKUNK tries to put
them on without flashing the world.

SKUNK: Nah, just thought I had a live one.

NOBLE: What did she do? Die?

SKUNK: Get this. There we were, naked in the lake.
Then she saw a gull and thought it was a hawk and,
well – *zoom* – she was out of the water and racing
down the beach after the thing so fast, just a
blonde white butt flashing in the sun as she
streaked through a patch of poison ivy. All the time
yelling, "Hawk feathers! I have to get hawk
feathers." So there I was, standing in the water
feeling ... more and more deflated, if you know
what I mean.

NOBLE: Hey, I can dig. Been there, done it, still
living the experience.

SKUNK: Talk about the one that got away. You're new
around here, aren't you?

NOBLE: It's been a few years since I've been new anywhere, but I just got back from out west. Did you know they have takeout beer there?! Anyways, Noble's my name, dancing's my game.

SKUNK: My handle's Skunk. You a dancer, too?

NOBLE: Yep.

SKUNK: Traditional?

NOBLE: Nope.

SKUNK: Grass?

NOBLE: Nope?

SKUNK: Fancy?!

NOBLE: Yep. Have bustle, will travel.

SKUNK: Seriously?! How old are you?

NOBLE: Thirty-eight. Got a problem with that?

SKUNK: Hey, no man; thirty-eight's cool – my father's almost thirty-eight – but isn't that a little old to be doin' fancy? I'm not saying you're old or anything, but thirty-eight is a bit long in the tooth for all that hopping and whirling.

NOBLE: The teeth may be long, but they can still bite, kiddo. Thirty-eight's not old. A lot of people can do things when they're a lot older than that. I'm in my prime.

SKUNK: Take it easy, I didn't mean anything like that. I've only been dancing a few years myself, but I thought when you got older, you usually went to grass, then traditional.

NOBLE: Hey, I'm a rebel. Don't forget it. Too old …

Angrily, wanting to show his fitness, NOBLE bends over and picks up the metal poles from his ancient tent.

Almost instantly he groans, in obvious pain. SKUNK rushes to his aid.

SKUNK: Hey, Noble, you okay?

NOBLE: Yeah, I'm okay. Just an old war wound.

SKUNK: You fought in a war?

NOBLE: Yep, married for five months.

SKUNK takes the poles from NOBLE.

SKUNK: No wonder. These things are heavy. How old is this tent?

NOBLE: What's this thing you have with how old things are? It's as old as it is. No more. No less.

SKUNK: My tent weighs a little over four pounds. You should get a new one.

NOBLE: Listen, me and this tent go way back. If this tent could talk ... I'd be on some serious drugs.

SKUNK: Do you need some help setting it up?

NOBLE: No, I don't need any help, but if you want to lend a hand, I wouldn't argue with you. The sooner we get this done, the quicker we can find a party.

SKUNK and NOBLE start to put the tent together. SKUNK spots something and recoils.

SKUNK: There's a dead squirrel in your tent.

NOBLE: So?

Scene Two

AMOS is getting his food stand together. It is a trailer-like structure with signs on it saying things like, Nish Chalet, Fortune Scones, Nee-Cheese Burgers, Corn Soup from the Ab-original Recipe, etc. PASHIK enters, looking depressed.

PASHIK: Hey, mister. You open?

AMOS: For a pretty girl like you, I could be, as long as it's not something complicated. I don't have the grills working yet.

PASHIK: I just want a pop and chips if you got them.

AMOS: That I do. Coming right up.

He runs into the trailer as PASHIK sits on the picnic table. He emerges almost instantly with two cans of pop and a bag of chips.

AMOS: Here you go, that'll be two dollars.

PASHIK: I only wanted one pop.

AMOS: I never let customers drink alone. Bad for business.

He opens both cans and gives her one. She raises it in a mock salute.

PASHIK: Cheers.

AMOS: *The Cosby Show.* Pretty girls shouldn't be so sad looking. What's wrong, your puppy die?

PASHIK: No, my social life.

AMOS: That's tough for a teenager, I hear. What's the problem?

PASHIK looks at him as if to say, "Why do you want to know?"

AMOS: Tell you what. Pretend this table is a bar, I'm a bartender, and these are whiskies. (*puts on a gravelly voice*) So, stranger, new in town? Now look, we don't want any trouble in this bar, so don't get into

27

any fights, okay? Or I'll have to call our sheriff,
Wyatt Burp.

PASHIK: Sir, what kind of medication are you on?

AMOS: (*in his normal voice*) Just life. Come on, what's
your problem? Old people like me are good
listeners. With or without hearing aids.

PASHIK: I want to go to Connecticut.

AMOS: You must want some clam chowder real bad.
What's in Connecticut?

PASHIK: Have you ever heard of that big powwow
they hold in Hartford every fall? The one that has
over $500,000 in prize money?

AMOS: Schemitzun.

PASHIK: Bless you.

AMOS: No, that's the name of the powwow.
Schemitzun.

PASHIK: You've been there? Wow! That's where I
want to go. I want to dance, compete, win, and take
over the world.

AMOS: That's a lot of ambition for a little girl.

PASHIK: I am not a little girl, I'm ... a woman. And
that has nothing to do with going to Connecticut.
My mother just wants me to end up like her. Just
sitting around here for the rest of my life, doing
nothing, being nothing. Connecticut is calling my
name and I wanna be there to call back. There are
sometimes 200,000 people there, I hear.

AMOS: Yep, I know. Try and find a parking spot. How
old are you?

PASHIK: Me? I'm ... eighteen. Yep, eighteen.

AMOS: Shoot, you're practically old enough. I was on the road myself when I was your age.

PASHIK: That's what I say, so was my mother but she won't listen to me. But you're right, I am old enough to do what I want. She was practically pregnant with me when she was my age. (*gets an idea*) Hey, are you going this September? Connecticut, I mean. Could I get a ride? I'll help. I can cook, all that sort of stuff.

AMOS: Sorry. It's a little far for these old bones to travel these days.

PASHIK: I didn't think so. I'm beginning to think she's gonna win and I'll never get out of here.

SKUNK comes jogging in towards the food trailer, looking sweaty but fit.

SKUNK: Hey, Amos, how're they hanging? Could I get two Cokes, please?

AMOS: You got it.

AMOS goes inside for the pop, leaving SKUNK and PASHIK to notice each other.

SKUNK: (*to himself*) Oooh, what have we here. (*louder*) Hi.

PASHIK: Hi.

SKUNK: You from around here?

PASHIK: Uh-huh.

SKUNK: Nice place.

PASHIK: You going to Connecticut?

SKUNK: What?

AMOS re-enters with his pop.

AMOS: You can't be that thirsty. Why do you need two?

29

*SKUNK looks behind him as NOBLE comes staggering
into camp. He is covered in sweat and breathing
heavily. He falls against the trailer for support.*

PASHIK: Holy ... what happened to him?

SKUNK: That hill over there. We were out jogging, to
get loosened up for today's grand entry, and we
came to that hill. Strangest thing I ever saw. The
way he was breathing going up it sounded like a
one of those old-style trains revving itself up, steam
pouring from his ears, and I kept hearing him say,
"I think I can, I think I can."

AMOS: And did he?

NOBLE: (*raspy*) Damn right. I knew I could. I knew I
could.

PASHIK: Hey, mister, you better sit down.

NOBLE: Just a little winded, that's all.

*NOBLE sits with a thump. AMOS gives a can of pop
to NOBLE, who grabs it like a dying man would a
glass of water.*

SKUNK: I told you we should have just done a couple
of laps around the campground but ...

NOBLE: I'm just a little rusty. Leave me alone.

SKUNK: Want me to run back and get your truck?
It'll only take me a second.

NOBLE: I hate you.

PASHIK: Wow, I've never seen an elder pout before.

NOBLE: (*loudly*) I'm not an elder! (*turns quickly to
AMOS*) Not that I have anything against elders.

AMOS: That's okay, son, I remember when I quit
dancing. Went kicking and screaming, too. It's not
easy when your wind goes, is it?

30

NOBLE: You used to be a dancer?

AMOS: Oh, a million years ago. Way back before either of your times. I was dancing when dancing wasn't cool. When you're Skunk's age, you like to think you'll live forever and have a flat stomach and one chin till the day you die. But the years creep by and your breath with it.

NOBLE: You know each other?

AMOS: We've met. You know the powwow trail. I'm Amos.

NOBLE: Any man with a cold pop is a friend of mine. Name's Noble.

PASHIK: You feeling better, mister?

NOBLE: Told you I was just winded a bit.

SKUNK: I told him to take it easy. A man his age shouldn't –

NOBLE: Hey!

AMOS: Skunk, respect your elders.

NOBLE: I'm not an elder!

PASHIK: He's pouting again.

NOBLE: I am not – and who are you, anyway?

PASHIK: My name is Pashik.

NOBLE: Pashik? Like the number *1* in Ojibway?

PASHIK: That's me.

SKUNK: Your parents accountants or something? Who would name their kid after a number?

PASHIK: This coming from a guy named Skunk? And don't call me kid!

NOBLE: How'd you become Pashik? There's gotta be a story there.

PASHIK: I was born at one o'clock on the first. I was her first child and, well, Mom looks for all that symbolic stuff. She's into that.

AMOS: Well, got food to fix and fat to fry. Can't waste the day standing here working on my tan.

AMOS exits into his trailer.

SKUNK: (*to PASHIK*) So, like, does this place have taxis? We should be getting back.

NOBLE: I told you I don't need my truck and I certainly don't need a taxi. I'm not going anywhere. I happen to like it here. It's a comfortable table with a great view, I may even set up my sleeping bag on top here and let all these people eat off my belly. You just go home. I'll be okay.

SKUNK: You sure?

NOBLE gives him an evil glare.

SKUNK: Okay, I'm outta here.

PASHIK: Which way you going?

SKUNK: That way, I guess. Back to the campgrounds.

PASHIK: I know a shortcut.

SKUNK: Lived here long?

PASHIK: All my life, since I was born … nineteen years ago.

SKUNK: Then lead on.

He gives NOBLE a nudge.

SKUNK: (*to NOBLE*) Another live one, and I think this one knows the difference between a gull and a hawk.

NOBLE: Yeah, she's cute. I'm tempted to go after her myself.

SKUNK: Yeah right. But when we were running earlier, when we stopped as you were throwing up in the bushes, this old woman passed us in a car. I caught her checking out your behind when you were doubled over the ditch, just before you fell in. She was pretty hot looking for someone in her fifties. You should give her a shot.

NOBLE: I don't think so. Hey, Pashik, can I buy you a pop or something? Wanna hang out or something?

PASHIK: Sorry, can't. Promised I'd show Skunk the shortcut back. Thanks anyways. Besides, maybe you should take a nap or something.

NOBLE: (*to SKUNK*) Get out of here, take her with you.

SKUNK: Nice try though. Hope I'm still in there swinging when I'm your age. Catch you later.

SKUNK and PASHIK exit. NOBLE watches them go, a sad expression on his face.

NOBLE: Ah, young love. It's enough to make you sick.

He finishes the last of his pop. He tries to toss the empty can into a trash can beside the trailer, but misses badly.

NOBLE: Not even a lousy two points. (*looks up at the sky*) You can't even give me two lousy points. It's not even a real two points. For God's sake, it's a stupid garbage can two points. Don't I even rate that?!

He collapses on the picnic table as AMOS enters with a tray of bread-making materials.

33

AMOS: Hey, you thinking of taking a nap on my picnic table?

NOBLE: Just bury me under this table and I'll be fine. I'm told I'll make great fertilizer.

AMOS starts to make some dough.

AMOS: Something wrong, son?

NOBLE: Just the usual. I can't run or dance anymore like I used to. I hurt all over when I do. The sight of young love makes me sick. And I've got a sliver in my ass from your picnic table and I haven't got the energy to take it out.

AMOS: I see. Have you ever ridden a horse bareback?

NOBLE: What?

AMOS: Bareback. Have you ever ridden a horse bareback?

NOBLE: No, I always wear a shirt. Why?

AMOS: It's a great feeling. Nothing between you and your horse, everything relying on the strength of your legs to hold on. No matter how old you are, when you ride bareback, it always makes you feel young. No, I'm wrong. It doesn't make you feel young, it makes you feel ageless.

NOBLE: That's all fine and dandy, but I can't fit a horse in my pickup.

AMOS: You need to find something that will make you feel young. That's all. If you have to, do what white people do to feel young. Get one of them tummy tucks or something.

NOBLE: No, thank you, I'm a firm believer in embracing what the Creator has decided to give us. Ain't no need to spit in his face.

AMOS: Good attitude.

NOBLE: Sure could use something, though, to pick up my spirits.

AMOS: You'll find something. People always do.

NOBLE watches AMOS kneed the dough.

NOBLE: Making some bannock?

AMOS: Sorta. It's a special kind of bannock. I call them fortune scones.

NOBLE: Fortune scones?

AMOS: Got the idea in a Chinese restaurant. I fry them with little philosophical Indian sayings in the middle. People love them.

NOBLE: You're kidding?!

AMOS: No, it sells. White people will buy anything. Here, try one.

He hands a warm scone to NOBLE, who takes a bite, then pulls a strip of paper from the middle. He reads it.

NOBLE: "People who need people are the luckiest people."

AMOS: Sorry, had a girl working for me that was really into Streisand. Thought I got rid of all those ones. Try this one. They're supposed to give you some sort of direction in life.

NOBLE: Sort of like a vision quest in a bun, huh?

NOBLE bites into another one and reads the inscription.

NOBLE: "All that glitters is not gold, and all that's black is not coal." Oh, now that reeks with Native spirituality. I've heard this somewhere before.

AMOS: Doesn't mean it's not true. "Do unto others as you would have them do unto you," doesn't just apply to Christians. Just like "Let me not criticize my neighbour until I have walked two moons in his moccasins," doesn't just apply to Indians.

NOBLE: But what does this have to do with me?

AMOS: Hey, I just make 'em and bake 'em. Find another elder to interpret them.

SUMMER enters wearing even more jewellery, if that's possible. Every once in a while she scratches her ankles.

SUMMER: Oh goody, would it be possible to buy a buffalo burger from you? I usually don't eat red meat, but who am I to stand in the way of aboriginal enterprise. I am here to support you and your cause. So give me a buffalo burger and I will be proud to eat and digest it.

AMOS: That's very fine, young lady, but the grill won't be open for another hour or so.

NOBLE: Say, that's a lot of jewellery you got there. You just buy it?

SUMMER: Just some trinkets I picked up on my travels. (*realizes what she has said*) But I don't mean "trinkets" in a pejorative or racially exploitive sense, you understand ...

NOBLE: In a ... what?

AMOS: Here for the powwow, I gather?

SUMMER: Yes, isn't it exciting?

She scratches her ankles again.

AMOS: I'm quivering. Ah, young lady, you got something wrong with your ankles?

SUMMER: Poison ivy, I'm afraid. Wasn't watching where I was going.

NOBLE: Oh, so that was you. Sit down, please.

SUMMER: What time does the powwow start? I can hardly wait.

NOBLE: Usually around noon.

SUMMER: Oh goody!

NOBLE: I agree. Oh goody.

AMOS pulls out a pop and gives it to SUMMER.

AMOS: Anybody with that much enthusiasm deserves a pop on the house.

SUMMER: Oh meegwetch.

AMOS: (*surprised*) Meegwhat?!

SUMMER: (*in Ojibway*) Way ya ghee ko moan na nishnabin too wa ojibway. Bow ting. [*Yes, I have taken conversational Ojibway in the city for the last little while. How do I sound?*]

AMOS: Excuse me, but what was all that?

SUMMER: I was just telling you about my taking conversational Ojibway classes. Didn't you understand? How come you don't speak Ojibway?

AMOS: Probably because I'm Mohawk.

SUMMER: Oh, my ... I'm so sorry. That was just my white concept of pan-Indianism coming through. And just because it's Ojibway country doesn't always mean there's only Ojibways. (*in Mohawk*) Skon'nikon kriyonsten. Yah nonwenton are thansayawen'. [*A thousand apologies. It will never happen again.*]

AMOS: Mohawk, too, huh?

NOBLE: How about Cree?

SUMMER: (*in Cree*) Mootha mista-eh oma neethowan mytha ma-ah goo a pitch n-goo-chan. [*I'm not as good in Cree, but I'm trying.*] I figure that since I don't know what Nation I am, I'd better be prepared. Do you speak Cree?

NOBLE: Me? No. But I can hold my own in Ojibway and I'm still working on English. Amos?

AMOS: I know a dabbling of Mohawk, but I'm actually much better in French. (*with a teasing wink*) Voulez-vous couchez avec moi c'est soir?

NOBLE: In school, I picked up some Latin from the priests. I thought it was kind of fun. *In vino veritas.*

> *SUMMER is flabbergasted by all this. This is not what she expected.*

SUMMER: Wait a minute. This isn't how it's supposed to be!

NOBLE: Oops, kind of ruins the image, don't it?

AMOS: Miss ...

SUMMER: Summer.

AMOS: Nice name. Suits you. Come here and sit down.

> *She does as he says.*

AMOS: There is something you have to understand about Native people. Just because we're proud of who and what we are, doesn't mean we can't appreciate the rest of the world out there. I personally think there's no better food than a wild-rice casserole with deer meat. However, I also get a hard-on for a good lasagna. It doesn't have to be one or the other.

SUMMER: Oh, you are so wise.

AMOS: (*aside to NOBLE*) They love stuff like this.
(*to SUMMER*) So you understand?

SUMMER: Of course I do. I was being so silly. I mean,
you people are so adaptable. Just like the way we
have adopted tobacco, corn, and the potato, why
shouldn't you be able to enjoy some of the benefits
of our culture. It's so obvious.

AMOS: Very good. Summer, I'm Amos and this here
is Noble.

SUMMER: Noble?! Is that the English translation of
your Native name, like "Noble Warrior" or "Noble
Eagle That Flies Across the Blue Sky to Greet the
Coming Dawn"?

NOBLE: Actually ... No, that sounds good. I'll go with
that.

SUMMER: Are you a ... drummer?

NOBLE: No, a dancer.

SUMMER: A dancer! Wow!

*There are stars in SUMMER's eyes, stars that are
impossible for NOBLE to miss.*

NOBLE: Amos, you know what you were saying about
me finding something to make me feel young. I
think I just found it. (*to SUMMER*) So, this your
first powwow?

SUMMER: The first of many, I hope.

NOBLE: Look, I have to head back to the
campground, specifically my tent. Want to walk
with me? I can tell you all about the spiritual
meaning of my dances.

SUMMER: Oh, that would be so cool.

NOBLE: Bye, Amos.

AMOS: Later, Noble.

SUMMER: (*in Mohawk*) Onen ki'wahi. Nyawen ki'wahi tsisattokha'tsheriyo. [*Goodbye and thank you for your wisdom and kindness.*]

AMOS: Ditto.

NOBLE puts his arm around SUMMER as they walk off.

NOBLE: So how long have you been interested in Native people and powwows?

SUMMER: Ever since I started taking this course at university. The more I read and the more I studied Native people, I knew there was so much they could teach mc. And did you know I'm part Indian, too?!

NOBLE: Of course you are.

AMOS eats one of his fortune scones. He pulls out the fortune.

AMOS: "The real difference between white people and Native people is: Native people have a round dance; White people have a square dance." Ain't it the truth?

Scene Three

SUMMER and NOBLE walk out of the woods. They are talking animatedly.

NOBLE: And there I was, gun in my hand, back to the plains, taking a stand for what we believed in. The Dakotas were cold that time of year, but we AIMsters didn't feel the biting cold of the harsh Dakota winter as we faced incredible odds. And did I mention how poorly dressed we were against the

40

freezing bite of winter? Ah, Wounded Knee. F.B.I. bastards!

SUMMER: And you were at Oka, too. Wow!

NOBLE: S.Q. bastards.

SUMMER: This is so great. I have one question.

She pulls out her tape recorder and turns it on.

SUMMER: This is for my class. I can't believe how lucky I am to have met you. This is so great. Now, since you were at both of these pivotal moments in aboriginal history, I would love to hear your opinion on the socio-political implications of the events in respect to today's Indigena political agenda.

NOBLE: So would I.

JENNY enters from off the side where she has been listening.

JENNY: Somehow I think if it doesn't have beer or boobs, he doesn't have an opinion.

SUMMER: Oh, hello.

NOBLE: (*to SUMMER*) Stand behind me. Don't show fear. (*to JENNY*) You want something?

JENNY: A lot of things but nothing you can help me with. I'm just making sure all the dancers and drummers have registered for tomorrow. Have you?

NOBLE: Not yet. I've been busy.

JENNY: So I see.

NOBLE: (*to SUMMER*) Um, I've got to fill out some forms. Seems you can't be a dancer without doing the paperwork. I'll meet you back at the tent. Okay?

41

SUMMER: Okay. Don't be too long, I want to hear that story about you being an extra in *Dances with Wolves*.

NOBLE: Yeah yeah, sure, later. Bye.

SUMMER: Bye. (*to JENNY*) Nice to meet you.

JENNY: A pleasure. Watch out for snakes, it's been a bad year for them. Especially the big ones.

SUMMER, now extremely nervous, has her eyes glued to the grass. She walks as though she is on eggshells.

JENNY: *Dances with Wolves*, huh? Did you get Kevin's autograph? You sure do operate pretty quick. The powwow hasn't even started and you have your first groupie. I'm impressed.

NOBLE: Give me the form.

JENNY hands it to him, and he starts to fill it out.

JENNY: Oh, you can write!

NOBLE: (*lifts up his left fist*) Yeah, but my left is better. What is it with you? Ever since I got here you've been on my case. It's a little early for distemper season, isn't it?

JENNY stares at him. This unnerves NOBLE.

NOBLE: What? You gonna hit me?

JENNY: You're right. I have been riding you kinda hard and I don't even know you. Look, I'm sorry. It's just been a hell of a week.

NOBLE: That's better. A pretty face like yours shouldn't scowl. Could freeze that way.

JENNY: That would be the least of my problems. I've got a daughter that's giving me grief, and a powwow that's getting out of control. And on top of all this, I take it out on you just because you remind

42

me of some slime buckets I used to know ...
bringing back some old memories.

NOBLE: There's that word "old" again. I think the
world has become one big skipping record. And
are you saying I remind you of slime buckets? I
don't think I like that.

JENNY: No, I wasn't –

NOBLE: Look, lady, whatever your problems are, I'm
sorry, I almost care. Nobody should have to go
through whatever it was that made you such a wet
blanket. But as the saying goes, "We all have our
crosses to bear, and our battles to fight." You don't
see me dragging you into my little world, now do
you? I hope you'd do the same for me.

JENNY: I should have known. People like you are all
alike. Do you like being rootless, living on the wind,
staying just long enough to have a few meals,
maybe steal a kiss, then – *bang* – pack up and say
hello to the road? Having no family or friends?

NOBLE: I got family. My mom and the rest are back
home. I see them enough during the winter, but
summer is my time. Each place is like a television
show. You don't watch the same show over and over
again. You want variety – new shows, new plots, new
people. Why shouldn't life be the same? Reruns
bore me, lady. But I don't have to explain my life to
you. As a great man once said, "I yam what I yam."

JENNY: Listen, buddy, not all of us are given the
luxury of channel hopping. Some of us only get
one station, sometimes only one show, and we
make the best of it.

NOBLE: Get cable.

JENNY: I have such a beautiful and bright daughter. And there's so much I want her to be proud of, but it's so hard showing a pig-headed teenager the good stuff from the bad. They believe all that glitters is gold. But experience has taught me there's more fool's gold out there than real gold.

NOBLE: You've had a Fortune Scone, I see.

JENNY: Don't change the subject. This is a problem you have no understanding of, isn't it?

NOBLE: Sorry, no kids. But it sure sounded good.

JENNY: You finished with that form yet?

NOBLE hands it back to her.

NOBLE: Here you go. Enjoy.

JENNY takes the paper and turns to leave.

NOBLE: Aren't you going to wish me luck tomorrow?

JENNY: If you want. Good luck.

NOBLE: How about some emotion with that?

JENNY: Do I get to pick the emotion?

NOBLE: Something tells me you already have.

JENNY exits as NOBLE walks over to join SUMMER at his tent.

SUMMER: Who was that? I got the impression you knew her.

NOBLE: Only when I was a kid and had nightmares. Now where were we?

SUMMER: You were going to tell me some Indian legends. I do so want to get in touch with my ancestral heritage.

NOBLE: Okay, legends. Oh yes, legends. Okay. There were these three little pigs …

SKUNK comes running in, obviously excited.

SKUNK: Hey, Noble, I have to talk with you, man. It's important. Real important.

NOBLE: Later, I'm busy. I'm storytelling. And this story might have a happy ending for the storyteller.

SKUNK: But I need your advice. Come on, it won't take long. Please.

SUMMER: Sounds important. I'll leave you guys to have your meeting.

NOBLE: But ...

SUMMER: Can we meet later? Say ... later tonight. I hear storytelling is so much better by fire under the moonlight.

NOBLE: Yes, ma'am. Tonight. And I'll have a humdinger of a story waiting for you. Count on it.

SUMMER: Bye.

SUMMER exits, taking NOBLE's heart and other vital organs with her.

NOBLE: Okay, *Skunkus interruptus*, this had better be important. What's got your drawers in a knot?

SKUNK: It's Pashik.

NOBLE: That girl you went off with? What about her?

SKUNK: I need to borrow sixty bucks till tomorrow.

NOBLE: You interrupted me for that?!

SKUNK: Look, it's important. I need the money to get Pashik this silver bracelet she was eyeing at a booth. She really wants it and I want to impress her.

NOBLE: So what? Am I your father? You want an allowance now?

45

SKUNK: Come on, it's snagging time. I shouldn't have to remind an old-timer like you about it. And she is prime snag.

NOBLE: Maybe, but you're gonna have to do it on your own charms, sonny boy. The Bank of Noble is closed.

SKUNK: Hey, I'm a little short. Look, I'll pay you back tomorrow after I win first prize.

NOBLE: Hey, hey, hey, hold on there, buddy. Just what makes you think you're gonna win? There are other dancers at work here, you know. And some are determined to give you a run for your money.

SKUNK: Yeah, yeah, I know, but, hey, I won the past three competitions in a row. I'm not just hot, I'm positively glowing. So what about the sixty bucks?

NOBLE: I will not lend you sixty bucks because, buddy, somebody's got to take cocky little dancers like you down a peg. I plan to win that prize money and spend all that money hiring people to beat you up.

SKUNK: You mean, you're actually here to compete?

NOBLE: What the hell do you think my bustle and beads are for? A fashion statement? Yes, I'm here to compete and, yes, I'm gonna whip your ass.

SKUNK: Better men have tried.

NOBLE: I really don't want to hear about your personal life.

SKUNK: You want to play hardball, we'll play. I was always taught to respect my elders, but not when they're acting stupid. I'm almost half as old as you are. Remember the hill?

NOBLE: I was hungover.

SKUNK: What will your excuse be when you lose?

46

NOBLE: If I lose, it will be because I tripped over your dead body. Now get out of here, I've got things to do. I have got to save my energy for the competition.

SKUNK: Then it's a good thing Summer left. I have a feeling that woman, followed by a cold glass of water, would kill you.

NOBLE: Go play with your teenager.

SKUNK: Fine. Me and Pashik will do without your help. I'll see you on the powwow grounds.

NOBLE: Be prepared to be amazed.

SKUNK exits leaving the angry NOBLE behind.

NOBLE: I am not old and I can prove it. I still have all my teeth – most of them anyway. I can still see better than you can, when it's not too dark. I'm in my prime and proud of it. I could whip all you boys put together. Just wait till tomorrow. I'll show you the kind of fancy dancing thè Creator put you on this earth just to see. These legs and feet will be a blur, trust me. Old, huh? Old is a state of mind, and I'll show you I don't have a mind.

NOBLE enters his tent. If the tent had a door, he would have slammed it. A few seconds pass until we hear ...

NOBLE: (*loudly*) Oh, my back ...

Quietly PASHIK enters. It's obvious she's looking for SKUNK and stops at NOBLE's tent.

PASHIK: Hello, Noble, you in there?

NOBLE sticks his head out to see who it is.

NOBLE: Oh, it's you.

NOBLE groans and grunts as he crawls out of the tent.

NOBLE: I was doing push-ups in there. If you're looking for Skunk, he went off looking for you. That way, I think. Be careful, he's in a strange mood.

PASHIK: I needed to talk to someone and my mother's a lost cause. And well, you seemed so nice from this morning ...

NOBLE: Amos wasn't around?

PASHIK: Couldn't find him. Anyway, I need some advice.

NOBLE: I'll do my best. Shoot.

NOBLE looks through his duffle bag and is surprised.

NOBLE: Well, I'll be, I just found some beer. I guess the beer fairies were here. Want one?

PASHIK looks around nervously.

PASHIK: Sure, why not. We're all adults here, eh?

NOBLE: Better be, this is an adult-rated tent. So what's your problem?

PASHIK: I want to go to Connecticut.

NOBLE: I think it's in that direction.

PASHIK: I don't suppose you're going.

NOBLE: This time of year?! Are you kidding? The weather down there is damp enough to wilt your privates. I was down there years ago, I'm still finding moss in strange places.

PASHIK: See! Everybody's been there but me. I deserve a chance to go.

NOBLE: What's so special about Connecticut? I mean, really, American beer ...?

PASHIK: Are you kidding? It's some place outta here.
It's in another country, Indians from all over the
place. And I hear everybody is rich down there, at
this Hartford place. Rich Indians as far as you can
see. Something to do with casinos. I don't know
why everybody doesn't want to go down there.

NOBLE: Pashik, I've been almost every place and
sometimes the yellow brick road ain't all it seems to
be. Sometimes you're lucky if you can even find the
road.

PASHIK: I don't care. I still wanna go. You wouldn't
happen to be going there this fall, would you?
I mean, in time for that big powwow.

NOBLE: I wasn't planning on it.

PASHIK: (*big puppy-dog eyes*) I'd really like to go.

NOBLE: Then again ...

PASHIK: Really?

NOBLE: Really.

She gives NOBLE a big hug and NOBLE relishes it.

PASHIK: You are so wonderful.

NOBLE: I know. We're going to Connecticut!

PASHIK squeals and hugs NOBLE again.

NOBLE: Think of all the fun we're going to have
in ... Connecticut!

*She squeals with excitement and hugs NOBLE again,
who is enjoying this too much.*

NOBLE: I may not live through this trip.

PASHIK: Oh, thank you so much.

NOBLE: No, thank you. But one question. I thought you and what's-his-name, the boy wonder there, were making goo-goo eyes at each other.

PASHIK: Oh, please, not him. The last thing I need is another hormonal boy chasing me around.

NOBLE: Even better.

PASHIK: You know the type, guys just looking for memories, a notch on their belts. They'll say anything to get your attention.

NOBLE: I hate people like that.

PASHIK: That's the interesting thing about some of these powwows, you get the full spectrum. Occasionally you can find slime, or you can find the most amazing people in the world. Besides, it'll take somebody a lot smarter than that to get around my mother. And more important, he's not my type. Definitely not my type.

NOBLE: Oh, and just what is your type?

PASHIK: Oh, I don't know. I guess I like somebody more mature, somebody cooler, who's been around and has done things, you know? He'd have an edge to him. And he has to have a car or truck. And he has to be older. I've had enough of dating boys.

NOBLE: Nice choice of characteristics. You definitely are a woman of taste. And I like your attitude. Do what you want. Don't give in to pressure. Seize the day. You're only young once, make sure it's not full of regrets. (*to himself*) I hope he's watching.

PASHIK: Pardon?

NOBLE: Nothing. Well, maybe you'll find what you're looking for in Connecticut, or sooner if you know where to look. Would you like to see my eight-track collection?

PASHIK: Your what?

NOBLE: Never mind.

A dangerous thought occurs to NOBLE.

NOBLE: By the way, is your father a big man? A fast runner?

PASHIK: Don't have one. Just my mother.

NOBLE: Oh good, I can usually handle a mother. So where were we?

PASHIK: Oh, my mother would kill me if she knew a fancy dancer like Skunk was after me. She would blow a spleen.

NOBLE: Doesn't like us dancers, huh? (*has a thought*) Now, why does that sound so familiar?

PASHIK: No kidding. Supposedly my father was a fancy dancer who then – *bang* – took off. Mom never saw him again.

NOBLE moves closer. He's on the hunt.

NOBLE: Tragic.

PASHIK: I think you met her already. She's a member of the powwow committee here.

NOBLE: That's nice. Must be something about the water, but all the women I've met from here are so beautiful.

PASHIK: Yeah, like who else do you know from around here?

NOBLE: Don't laugh. You must have been just a baby the last time I was in town. But there was this beautiful girl I met, you're probably related to her.

PASHIK: What was her name?

NOBLE: Geez, that was so long ago. What a great
week we had together. There was a lot of fire in her
eyes, that's what attracted me to her. No, wait ...
I remember her name now. Nice guy, huh, almost
forgetting her name? Jenny ... it was Jenny.

*The smile fades off PASHIK's face and is replaced by
shock as she leans away from NOBLE.*

NOBLE: What? Did I say something wrong?

*It is a moment before PASHIK can bring herself to
speak. Her voice is hesitant and scared.*

PASHIK: Dad?!

*The fateful word slowly sinks into NOBLE's
consciousness. He falls to the ground, dazed.*

The lights go down.

ACT TWO

Scene One

The lights come up on NOBLE and PASHIK holding the same positions they had at the end of Act One. PASHIK is still wearing the look of stunned disbelief and NOBLE is practically comatose. Suddenly, PASHIK wheels about and races offstage in a desperate hurry. NOBLE lies there, not moving, not making a sound. A few seconds pass with no movement. SUMMER enters from the opposite direction that PASHIK exited. She walks along the stage, sees NOBLE on his back, stops for a moment, looks at him, puzzled. Then she looks up into the sky as if NOBLE is looking at something on his back, but she can't see anything.

SUMMER: Oh, he's being one with Mother Earth and Father Sky. Better not interrupt him.

She exits. NOBLE continues to lie there without moving or saying a word for a few seconds longer. Then SKUNK comes walking in casually. He, too, finds NOBLE in his prone position.

SKUNK: Hey, how's it going?

NOBLE: Fine.

SKUNK: Any particular reason you're down there?

NOBLE: Yes.

SKUNK looks at him for a moment longer, then shrugs.

SKUNK: Okay. Hey, I was thinking about our little discussion. If you're so sure you're gonna win, how'd you like to place a little bet on tomorrow's competition? If you wanna put your money where your mouth is.

No response from NOBLE.

SKUNK: Hey, you with me down there?

NOBLE: Can we talk about this a little later?

SKUNK: Ah, wanna think about it, huh? Good idea. I'll catch you later. Oh, by the way, I haven't been able to find Pashik. Have you seen her?

NOBLE points in the direction of PASHIK's exit.

SKUNK: Thanks. Be cool.

NOBLE gives him the thumbs-up sign. SKUNK exits and NOBLE continues to lie there till AMOS happens by.

AMOS: Hey.

NOBLE: Hey.

AMOS: You have nice boots.

NOBLE: Thanks.

AMOS: Comfy?

NOBLE: Not really.

AMOS: Is this, like, an Ojibway thing?

NOBLE: Amos, how do you say "father" in Mohawk?

AMOS: Rugnee.

NOBLE extends his arm, indicating that he wants help getting up. AMOS grabs his arm and helps him get vertical.

NOBLE: In Ojibway it's O'oos.

AMOS: Now that's something I've always wanted to know.

NOBLE: Rugnee, O'oos, Dad, Daddy, pop. Poppa Noble.

AMOS: I'm noticing a theme here.

NOBLE: I just found out I'm a father.

AMOS: Well, congratulations, my boy. I didn't even know you had a lady. Is the baby okay? I mean healthy.

NOBLE: She looked healthy.

AMOS: Wonderful. She? A little girl! You must be so proud. How much did she weigh?

NOBLE: About 120 pounds, I think. It was hard to tell; she was wearing baggy clothes.

AMOS: That's a big baby. The poor mother.

NOBLE: I just discovered Pashik is my daughter! The Noble Poppa. Oh God …

AMOS: Really!? She must have her mother's looks.

NOBLE: I can't be a father. Is this the face of a father?

AMOS: Hey, take it easy. Kids are good. I have five of my own. They're all grown up now and spread all over the place, but they're still my kids. Don't be afraid, embrace it. Pashik seems very nice. You could do a lot worse.

NOBLE: You don't understand, I don't know anything about being a father. I never knew mine. I grew up with just my mother and two brothers. You need training for something like this.

AMOS: Nope. Raising kids is baptism under fire. And Pashik is a bit old for you to be talking about raising her. She's pretty well raised. Where's Pashik now?

NOBLE: She ran off in that direction.

AMOS: So what are you going to do now?

NOBLE: (*pointing in the opposite direction*) Run off in that direction?

AMOS gives him a stern stare.

NOBLE: Just a suggestion.

AMOS: Who's the mother?

NOBLE: Her name was Jenny. Geez, I haven't seen her in, geez, close to twenty years or so.

AMOS: Don't you think you'd better find her? It's good manners in situations like this.

NOBLE: I wouldn't know where to find her.

AMOS: This is just a guess, but Pashik might know. That would be a good place to start.

NOBLE: Do I have to? I mean, what's done is done. No use crying over spilled milk, right?

This time, NOBLE gets a stern word.

AMOS: Noble ...

NOBLE: Okay, okay. I'll see what I can do.

AMOS: A child makes mistakes. A man corrects them.

NOBLE: Another Fortune Scone?

AMOS: No, experience.

AMOS and NOBLE leave through separate exits, and the stage is bare for a moment. Then from the edge of the stage, NOBLE sticks his head out to see if AMOS has left. Once he sees the coast is clear, he runs to his tent and starts stuffing all his stuff into his duffle bag.

He quickly tries to take his tent down, but is in so much of a hurry that he only succeeds in knocking the thing down and making a mess. He starts throwing everything into the tent and picks up the corners of the tent to carry like dishes in a tablecloth.

JENNY enters and watches him for a moment from the side. She shakes her head in disbelief as she watches things fall out of the tent as NOBLE attempts to carry the whole thing over his shoulder. He comically keeps picking things up and stuffing them back in the tent. As he makes his way across the stage, he bumps into JENNY.

NOBLE: Hey, babe, you got your wish. I am out of here. Have a nice powwow, keep my entrance fee, don't spend it all in one place. I'll write if I get work.

NOBLE is almost offstage when JENNY speaks.

JENNY: Hello, Noble.

NOBLE: (*singing*) "You say hello, I say goodbye. Goodbye, goodbye ..."

JENNY: It's been a long time.

NOBLE: Yeah, a good fifteen minutes. I've been told I grow on people. Gotta go, bye.

JENNY: Pashik is my daughter.

NOBLE freezes in his tracks. His tent drops with a thud.

JENNY: It's true. Pashik is my daughter. I'm Jenny, remember?

NOBLE: It figures.

JENNY: I didn't recognize you.

NOBLE: Jenny.

JENNY: You look so … different.

NOBLE: You lost the glasses.

JENNY: Contacts. You don't have a moustache anymore.

NOBLE: Tent fire. You've put weight on.

JENNY: You've let your hair grow.

NOBLE: You've gotten old.

JENNY: You've gotten ugly.

NOBLE: Just like old times, huh? So I guess Pashik told you.

JENNY: Yeah, but I knew before. Remember the form I asked you to fill out? I finally looked at the name.

NOBLE: So, how've you been?

JENNY: Busy. Going somewhere?

NOBLE tries to kick the tent aside.

NOBLE: This? I was just taking it down to the lake to give it a good rinsing. Nothing worse than a musty tent.

JENNY: My God, that's the same tent we …

NOBLE: What can I say, it's my lucky tent.

JENNY: On second thought, other than the moustache and hair, you really haven't changed much, you know. Everything's the same, right down to the slouch.

NOBLE straightens up immediately.

NOBLE: Well, I'm flattered you remember so much about me. It's nice to know I can make an impression.

JENNY: Oh, you made an impression, all right – an eight-pound, four-ounce one.

NOBLE: Leave them with a bang, I always say.

JENNY: I've always wanted to leave you with an impression, too.

JENNY nails NOBLE with a quick, powerful and painful punch. NOBLE goes down like a sack of potatoes.

JENNY: Think you'll remember me this time?

NOBLE: I see you're a little angry.

JENNY: I loved you, you know. I really did. And I think you knew that. That's why you left so quickly, didn't you?

NOBLE: Oh, Jenny, that was so long ago. Who knows what kids do. We were twenty years old.

JENNY: That is no excuse.

NOBLE: You knew what I was like. I never hid anything. I was as me as me can get, and if you fell in love with that, then that was your problem, not mine.

JENNY: You don't leave a pregnant woman behind.

NOBLE: I didn't know you were pregnant. We only knew each other for a week. Not even one week. Six days.

JENNY: You can remember how many days it was exactly, but you didn't …

NOBLE: Well, that's just how my schedule usually runs. Six days then there's another powwow somewhere. Hey, if it ain't broke …

JENNY punches him again and NOBLE eats more dirt.

NOBLE: Enough already. I get the point.

JENNY: You know, when I was nineteen, I believed in three things. I believed disco sucked, and I was right. Secondly, I swore I would never turn into my mother. Okay, I'll admit the jury's still out on that one. And finally, I thought I could change you. Well, so much for that one.

NOBLE: Oh, give me a break. You know how many times I've heard that? I'm me. Get used to it. I didn't try to change you or any other woman, but for some strange reason they always want to change me. Is this a female thing?

JENNY: Sometimes we get the urge to clean up messes. So, got any other kids?

NOBLE: Nope, don't think my heart could take it. This one just about killed me. Came damn close once when I got married.

JENNY: You were married?

NOBLE: Yep. It's what's called a marriage of convenience. I was conveniently drunk when I got married. But a couple months later we sobered up, saw each other in the light and, well, that was over quick.

JENNY: Why am I not surprised? Well, in case you might care, Pashik's a good kid. A little headstrong sometimes and likes to fight ...

NOBLE: She must get that from you.

JENNY: She can also be lazy and want to take the easy way out.

NOBLE: Well, look at the time. It's been a slice, Jenny. You do real good work, but like the noble hawk, I've got to fly.

NOBLE gathers up his tent.

JENNY: You don't even want to talk to your own daughter.

NOBLE: Oh, Jenny, why? What good would it do? I'd just make things worse. It's better if I leave.

NOBLE turns to leave, but JENNY intercepts him.

JENNY: I wouldn't move so fast if I were you.

NOBLE: You want to see fast, just wait a few minutes till I get to the truck.

JENNY: Oh, I've got a few minutes, I've got all the time in the world. So do you. And your truck won't help.

NOBLE: No comprendez, señorita.

JENNY holds up a distributor cap and dangles it in front of NOBLE.

NOBLE: My distributor cap. What did you do to my truck?

JENNY: There are two things I want from you before you disappear into the sunset again. A disappearing act is only interesting the first time.

NOBLE grabs the cap.

NOBLE: Yes, but you just gave me the magic wand. Hocus-pocus, I'm outta here.

He smiles as he moves the distributor cap out of her reach.

JENNY: Not so fast there, Houdini. That's not much good without the spark plugs, or your carburetor. Now is it?

NOBLE: My spar ... my carb ... You've done this before, haven't you?

JENNY: A single mother has to be resourceful. I'm quite handy around the house. I can build one, then clean it.

NOBLE: You're not the giggly teenager I remember.

JENNY: Most of us grow up. First of all – and I don't believe I'm saying this – I want you to get to know Pashik. Personally I couldn't care less if you disappeared into a big black hole, tent and all, but she's always wondered about you and she deserves – as much as I hate the idea – she deserves the chance to talk with you.

NOBLE: What's the second thing?

JENNY: I want seventeen years back child support.

NOBLE: Seventeen years?! You're kidding! That must be … thousands?

JENNY: It is. Now, for the sake of argument, let's say I got you to pay me $200 per month for Pashik, and that's letting you off cheap, buddy. So she just turned seventeen two months ago …

NOBLE: She told Skunk she was nineteen.

JENNY: Yeah, and the federal government is serious about settling all land claims. As I was saying, just to show there's no hard feelings, those extra two months are on the house. So, doing the math – can you tell I'm enjoying this? – doing the math is two hundred dollars times twelve times seventeen. When you work it out that comes out to exactly $40,800. Now that's a nice tidy sum. Cash please.

JENNY holds out her hand, palm up.

NOBLE: (*swallowing hard*) Forty thousand …
(*he coughs*)

JENNY: And eight hundred dollars – $40,800. Right now, please. I'm waiting.

NOBLE starts to rummage around in his pocket. He pulls out something and offers it to JENNY.

NOBLE: Chiclet?

JENNY: Only if it's made out of gold.

NOBLE: No, lint. I think I have some Canadian Tire money in the back of the truck. I can go count it and –

JENNY: I said cash.

NOBLE: Will you take an I.O.U.?

JENNY: I did, seventeen years ago. Think of it as aboriginal karma.

NOBLE: $40,800. Now where am I suppose to get that kind of money? That's a lot of powwow dancing. I don't think I could make that much if I won every powwow this summer.

JENNY: Not my problem. I have errands to run. I know I'll be seeing you later.

JENNY exits.

NOBLE: $40,800. That's my beer money for a year!

Scene Two

SUMMER and SKUNK are at AMOS's food stand. SUMMER is talking excitedly, overwhelming SKUNK as he eats a hamburger.

SUMMER: And he said he'd take me with him all over the country. What better way to finish my thesis than powwow hopping. Isn't that a fantastic idea? We'll be dancing over here and singing over there.

So many Indians, and so little time. Oh, I'm sorry, I mean Native, aboriginal, First Nations, indigenous people. I've just got to stop saying the word "Indian." After all, we're not called Indians anymore, are we? (*slaps her own wrist*) Bad Summer, bad Summer. Will you be going too? I mean, we could all camp together, sing forty-niner songs, go to ceremonies together. You and Noble could do that greeting-the-sun, morning-ritual thing of yours. It will be wonderful, won't it? Tell me a legend.

SKUNK: Amos!

AMOS emerges with a plate of fortune scones and puts it on the picnic table.

AMOS: Coming. Here, I brought some fortune scones. Dig in and let the future be told.

They all grab a scone and take a bite.

SKUNK: "Never trap on another person's trapline."

AMOS: "Eat, drink, and be merry, for tomorrow they may put you on a reserve." (*to SUMMER*) What does yours say?

SUMMER: "Check the authentic Native totem pole for a Made in Korea label." Oh, thank you, I will treasure it forever.

AMOS: Okay, if you want, but you'll be the only woman on your block treasuring mouldy bread. If you want my advice, just eat the damn thing. You should be more particular about the things you treasure.

SUMMER: You are just so wise.

SKUNK: Shoot, I could have told you that.

AMOS: Yeah, but it sounds better coming from a sixty-year-old man than a twenty-year-old boy. Advice is like fine wine, the older it is, the better it tastes.

SUMMER: Wow!

AMOS: (*to SKUNK*) See.

NOBLE comes running in, looking anxious.

NOBLE: Hey Summer, you got a car?

SUMMER: Of course I do. Why?

NOBLE: Go get it. We're leaving.

AMOS: I thought you had a truck.

NOBLE: I did ... I ... gave it to Pashik.

SUMMER: Who's Pashik?

SKUNK: I've seen your truck; poor Pashik.

AMOS: That was very nice of you, Noble.

NOBLE: Thanks, let's go.

SUMMER: But what about the powwow?

SKUNK: Yeah, we dance in a few hours.

AMOS: Is something wrong?

NOBLE: Everything's great. Hurry up, Summer.

SUMMER: But I want to see the powwow.

NOBLE: The ... um ... cosmic vibes aren't right. The ectoplasmic sweetgrass of creation said, "Move on." And I heard the owl call my name. Come on, let's move.

SKUNK: Wait a minute. You're blowing town, aren't you? After all this big talk about taking me on, you're running out.

NOBLE: Skunk, you don't understand what's going on –

SKUNK: All I'm seeing is your butt going in the opposite direction of the grounds. You're scared of me, aren't you?

NOBLE: Am not.

SKUNK: Are too.

NOBLE: Fine, I'll meet you at the dancing grounds for grand entry. Then we'll separate the men from the boys.

SKUNK: And what about that bet?

AMOS: What bet?

NOBLE: Name it.

SKUNK: Five hundred dollars. Too much?

NOBLE: Are you kidding?! That's the smallest amount anybody's wanted from me today. It's a bet.

They shake and NOBLE turns around and runs with SUMMER.

AMOS: Bye, Summer, Noble.

NOBLE turns around and quickly gives the Vulcan hand sign.

NOBLE: Live long and prosper. Bye.

NOBLE exits with SUMMER.

AMOS: I think somebody's drum is a little too tight. I wonder what's shaking that man's rattle. Oh well, Skunk, do you want another burger? On the house?

AMOS offers SKUNK a hamburger.

SKUNK: Sure. How do you stay in business giving away free food like this?

AMOS: Low overhead. Most of the meat I sell is roadkill.

SKUNK spits up a mouthful of hamburger.

Scene Three

NOBLE is hurrying SUMMER to the tent area. He quickly starts to gather up his belongings.

SUMMER: I have a question. Is it really proper to be betting on dancing?

NOBLE: Of course not. I'm surprised Amos didn't cuff him upside the head. Skunk's in it for the ego and the money.

SUMMER: But don't you dance for competition money?

NOBLE: To get me to the next powwow sure. I also do traditional powwows where there's no money. Skunk dances for the money. I dance because I'm a dancer and I'll always be one. It's part of me. That's why I'm still doing it at my age.

SUMMER: Then why did you bet him?

NOBLE: Because I didn't have time to argue. And when he comes to collect, we're going to be a distant memory burning gas to the dark side of the moon.

SUMMER: Do we really have to leave?

NOBLE: I know where there's some petroglyphs along the way.

SUMMER: Really?!

NOBLE: We can stop and you can tape them with that thing of yours.

SUMMER: My tape recorder? How do you tape petroglyphs?

NOBLE: I don't know. You're the student. You figure it out. Where's your car?

67

SUMMER: There. It's the Thunderbird. I thought it was wonderfully symbolic.

NOBLE: Go get it. We're on a deadline.

SUMMER: Why so fast? You'd think the Devil was after you. Do the Ojibway have a devil? And, if so, is it in the heaven/hell concept, or if not, is there an equal –

NOBLE: The car, Summer, the car?!

SUMMER: Oh yeah. I got to pack up my stuff, too. I'll be back in a few minutes.

SUMMER exits and NOBLE finishes packing everything up. Quietly at a distance, PASHIK and SKUNK walk by. NOBLE looks up in time to see them kiss. NOBLE reacts and hides behind a bush.

SKUNK: I love your eyes.

PASHIK: You do?

SKUNK: And your nose and your chin and your lips …

NOBLE: (*to himself*) Oh, please.

SKUNK leans forward and kisses PASHIK. NOBLE reacts.

PASHIK: Thank you.

SKUNK: No, thank you. To me you're something really special and I'm really glad I found you. I really mean it with every sincere fibre in my body. Really.

PASHIK: You know, at first I wasn't interested in you. But now that I've got to know you, you're okay. Especially since you said you'd take me to Connecticut.

SKUNK: I would do anything for you.

68

PASHIK: Really?

SKUNK: Really.

PASHIK: Oh wow.

SKUNK: I've got to get suited up for grand entry. Will
you be watching?

*PASHIK nods her head vigorously. SKUNK gives her a
token of his affection for her to wear.*

SKUNK: Then, I'll be dancing for you.

NOBLE: That little skunk has all my lines.

*They kiss and SKUNK exits. PASHIK watches him go,
love in her eyes. NOBLE comes out of the bushes.*

NOBLE: Pashik ...!

PASHIK wheels about, startled.

PASHIK: What do you want?

NOBLE: What was all that with Skunk?

PASHIK: You were spying on me?

NOBLE: It's a campground. Everybody spies.

PASHIK: Leave me alone.

NOBLE: What are you doing kissing a guy like that?
And what's this about him taking you to
Connecticut? You can't be serious.

PASHIK: I can, too. What's wrong with Skunk? Now
that I've got to know him, he's kind of cute.

NOBLE: He's trouble. Trust me, I know.

PASHIK: You never met him before today. How can
you know?

NOBLE: Easy. He's me. Or what I was twenty years
ago. He's so much like me I had to check my

driver's licence just to make sure I was me. And you're just like your mother. Stay away from him.

PASHIK: It's my life.

NOBLE: You're seventeen. You have no life. You're too young to go running off with a guy like him.

PASHIK: Says who?

NOBLE: I do, young lady. You just turn yourself around and, um ... go to your room, without any supper either. Yeah, that sounds good, and ... and ... stay there till school starts.

PASHIK: Next month?!

NOBLE: Yes. And ... and brush your teeth.

PASHIK: And just who do you think you are? My father? Sorry, it don't work that way. As far as I'm concerned, you're just a biological donor and you have about as much say in my life as I have in yours. Stay out of my life till you've taken part in it.

NOBLE: I'm just ... concerned.

PASHIK: Concerned, huh? Looks like you're packing up and leaving.

NOBLE looks guilty.

PASHIK: Have a good trip.

PASHIK exits.

NOBLE: Nice going. Do any better and she'd take an axe to you.

SUMMER runs in.

SUMMER: Okay, everything is packed.

NOBLE: Great. The sooner I'm outta here, the sooner life can get back to normal.

SUMMER: We'd better hurry. The car is running.

70

NOBLE: Running?! Did you say I'm running? I'm not running. I've just decided to let life continue as if I'd never been here.

SUMMER: What are you talking about?

NOBLE: Um, nothing.

SUMMER: Are you sure we can't stay? I'd really like to hear the drum.

NOBLE: Scum? Did you say I was scum? I am not scum. I'd make a terrible father. It don't take a genius to see that.

SUMMER: What's going on here? I'm lost. Is this some sort of aboriginal breakdown?

NOBLE: Never mind. Let's get out of here. (*he looks*) Hey, who are those two cops by your car?

SUMMER: Oh that's Fred and Howard. They say they're special constables. What does that mean?

NOBLE: That means they're reserve cops. What did they want?

SUMMER: I told them we were leaving and they wanted to meet you. They said something about them being the brothers of somebody named Jenny. They said you'd know what they meant, something about the village having only one road out and they'd be watching until Jenny got what was coming to her. And they carry hollow-tip bullets. What ever that means. I was wondering if this was some sort of a symbolic method of communication without actually saying anything concrete.

NOBLE: Oh, you'd be surprised how much is in that message. How wide would you say that lake is?

SUMMER: About two miles maybe.

71

NOBLE: Sure wish I could swim. Maybe if I got a running start ...

SUMMER: I don't suppose you'd like to tell me what's going on?

NOBLE: Just a very resourceful and determined woman. I don't suppose you have a spare $40,800 you could lend me.

A voice booms over the campground.

ANNOUNCER: Ladies and gentlemen, grand entry in half an hour and the dance competitions will follow. Get your dancing moccasins on. It's powwow time!

NOBLE: Plus five hundred dollars.

SUMMER: Um, my car's running. What do you want me to do?

NOBLE: Run me over.

SUMMER: Is that a joke?

NOBLE: Summer, just leave me alone. Let me be.

SUMMER: Okay, if that's what you want.

NOBLE: That's what I want.

SUMMER: Fine. I'll go talk to Fred and Howard.

NOBLE: Will you quit saying things like that. I am not a coward!

SUMMER exits.

NOBLE: Mommy said I'd suffer when I had kids of my own.

Scene Four

JENNY is buying a Fortune Scone from AMOS.

AMOS: There you go. Enjoy.

JENNY: I love these things, and they're cheaper than a fortune teller.

AMOS: And they're also more fattening than a fortune teller.

JENNY: What isn't?

She bites into it and pulls out the fortune.

JENNY: Let's see. It says, "Beware of unusually coloured snow."

AMOS: Truer words were never spoken.

A buzzer is heard.

AMOS: My fryer. Gotta go.

AMOS disappears into the trailer as NOBLE rushes up.

NOBLE: Hey, Jenny, we got a problem.

JENNY: We? Did I hear a we? My, aren't we plural lately? You don't have a problem, you have 40,800 of them. (*laughs*) "We have a problem." Oh that's rich. And I will be, too! Ha! I'm so funny.

NOBLE: It's about Pashik.

JENNY: What about her?

NOBLE: Prepare yourself. It's serious. She's planning to run off with Skunk.

JENNY: Again?

NOBLE: Again? What again? She's going to leave with Skunk! Hello, anybody at home in there?

JENNY: Relax. Now who's this Skunk fellow?

NOBLE: Well, excuse me for being concerned. I didn't realize parenting was such a laid-back profession.

JENNY: Just point him out to me.

NOBLE visually searches the crowd, finds him, and points him out.

NOBLE: That's him, the one in the yellow.

JENNY: He's cute.

NOBLE: What is this with you. Your daughter – our daughter – the fruit of our loins ...

JENNY: Oh, please, don't put it that way.

NOBLE: She's going to run off with that guy and all you can say is, "He's cute"?

JENNY: I said the same thing about you way back when.

NOBLE: Exactly, and look where it got you.

JENNY: Pop a Valium. Pashik threatens this all the time. You get used to it. She sets her eyes on some hot-lookin' kid and the stars flash, the heart pounds, hormones run and – *bang* – she sees a way to get away from Mommy dearest. It'll take more than some pubescent hotshot dancer to get the best of me. Got my money yet?

NOBLE: Forget your money! You're just gonna leave it like that? You're a cold-hearted woman.

JENNY: No, I'm a practical mother. Which one's his car?

NOBLE: His car? Uh, that one. Why?

JENNY: Oh god, he drives a Duster. So much for taste. But, as you say, it doesn't pay to take chances.

NOBLE: So?

JENNY: I think I'll mosey over there and just add to my spark plug collection. Dusters have good alternators, too, don't they?

NOBLE: Is that your answer for everything?

JENNY: Men have two points of pride. One is on wheels, the other is on their body. I can remove either.

NOBLE: You win.

JENNY: Never underestimate the intelligence or abilities of a mother. Especially one who's been there, done it, and knows what to expect.

AMOS comes out, wiping his hands. JENNY takes a wrench and screwdriver out of her purse.

JENNY: And most importantly, a mother is always prepared. Boy Scouts could learn a lot from us.

JENNY exits.

NOBLE: (*to AMOS*) I'm beginning to remember what I saw in her. Some women have beauty, some have smarts, and some have style. And some have my carburetor.

AMOS: Sure does seem like a fine woman. What does she make you feel?

NOBLE: Like they could have been my future.

AMOS: I always thought guys like you didn't care about the future.

NOBLE: Maybe the future doesn't care about guys like me.

AMOS: Noble, my boy, I think you're beginning to tap into the big circle of life. You can dance all you want, sing till the birds come home, but unless you

75

take a look at the big picture and look for yourself in it, the dancing and singing are useless.

NOBLE: Boy, Summer was right, you are good at this. Where'd you pick that up?

AMOS: The Elder Handbook. Where do you think I got it? Life, my boy, life. The more you live, the more knowledge you have to fall back on. Being an elder is no mystical thing, it's just the ability to draw wisdom from your and others' past experiences. That's the difference between being an elder and just being old. That's a beautiful daughter you have there. Good dancer, too, from what I've heard.

NOBLE: She's a dancer?

AMOS: Yep, must be your crumby zones. Most men in your position would be excited having a daughter like that. I have five daughters and I love them dearly. I always wanted a son, too, but the Creator didn't see fit. But that's okay. My girls are the best women in the world to me. And from the little I know her, she's already got a lot of you in her.

NOBLE: She does, doesn't she?

AMOS: Of course she does. And it would sure be a help if there was somebody there to help her, someone who's already done everything she wants to do. But being a teenager she probably wouldn't listen anyway, so I could be talking through my hat. Better just ignore everything I've just said.

NOBLE: You're a lot of help.

AMOS: You have good days and you have bad days. You try carrying sixty years of doing things in your head and let's see you get everything straight. Sorry, Noble, you got to do this on your own.

NOBLE: I tried earlier but I just screwed it up.

AMOS: You two have seventeen years to catch up on. That's a hell of a bridge to build so quickly. You got to move slowly. Take your time.

NOBLE: How do you talk to somebody ... somebody that's your daughter? I don't know what to say. Sure could use a beer. Got any?

AMOS: No. And if I did I wouldn't give you any. I said you got to do this on your own.

NOBLE: Any advice first?

AMOS: Don't ask me, ask the Fortune Scone.

AMOS hands him one and just as NOBLE is about to break it in half, AMOS holds out a hand.

AMOS: One dollar, please.

NOBLE: But you were giving these out for free, earlier.

AMOS: You have to learn to start paying your way sometime. Everything costs something – except love.

NOBLE pays AMOS, then bites off the tip of the scone and pulls out the message.

NOBLE: "Life is a circle. Try not to get lost."

NOBLE exits.

Scene Five

PASHIK, wearing a shawl, is practising a few tentative dance steps to the sound of the drum as JENNY approaches.

JENNY: Hey.

PASHIK: Hey.

JENNY: Your heart's not in it.

PASHIK: Got things on my mind.

JENNY: Things like a boy named Skunk.

PASHIK: (*looking up*) You didn't.

JENNY holds up a variety of car parts.

PASHIK: Mom, you can't keep stealing car parts from boys I like. We're running out of room. Our basement looks like a Rent-a-Wreck exploded.

JENNY: You know the plan. When we get enough parts, we'll build our own car.

PASHIK: Mom! When people say they're saving up to get a car, they usually mean saving up money, not car parts.

JENNY: I'm just eliminating the middle person. Next time, date somebody with power windows, okay?

PASHIK: Maybe there won't be a next time.

JENNY: Yes, there will. You just wait. There'll be another Skunk before I know it. Always remember: so many men, so few brain cells. Why can't you date somebody here? This place is crawling with boys.

PASHIK: You know as well as I do – thanks to Granny and Grandpa who had fourteen kids – I'm related to everybody within a four-mile radius. And there's nobody here I want to date anyway.

JENNY: I know what you're going through. I grew up here, too. You are only seventeen –

PASHIK: Oh, not this again.

JENNY: Yes, this again. First, you're only seventeen. Second, your final year of high school starts next month and I won't have you jeopardizing that. And third, I'd miss you too much.

PASHIK: What?

JENNY: You heard me.

PASHIK: No, I didn't.

JENNY: I said I'd miss you.

PASHIK: You would not.

JENNY: I would.

PASHIK: All mothers say that kind of stuff.

JENNY: That's probably because it's true. Look, all I
want is one more year of fighting over the
television, going shopping with you, yelling at you
to turn down that music of yours. Next year you're
eighteen, and you'll be legal enough to do most
things. So just give me another year as your mother.
That's all I ask.

PASHIK: But there's so much happening this summer
that I don't want to miss. And Connecticut …

JENNY: Well, I can't argue with your enthusiasm. Tell
you what, if you're good this weekend, and next
week, maybe we'll find a way to go to the Otter
Lake powwow.

PASHIK: I thought I was grounded?

JENNY: Being grounded can have two different
meanings. The other is knowing who you are and
where you belong. That's the better view of being
grounded. Do you know what one of my favourite
memories of you is? It was the time you were
dancing at that powwow up by Sudbury. Remember
where the dancers danced on that big dock thing
over the water? And remember how you were
dancing so hard and so fast, your little legs going
this way and that way, but you weren't looking
where you should have been and you fell – *splash* –

79

right into the lake. When you came out you looked like a brightly coloured, drowned rat. And you were crying so much. Boy, I laughed.

PASHIK: Mom! My costume was ruined!

JENNY: Yeah, but it was funny.

PASHIK: What about Noble?

JENNY: What about him?

PASHIK: What should I do about him?

JENNY: He's your father. Talk to him. Knowing him as I do, he's trying his damnedest to get out of town. Better grab him quick or he'll disappear for another eighteen years.

PASHIK: I don't want to talk with him.

JENNY: You sure?

PASHIK: Definitely.

JENNY: Sweetie, that part of your life is yours. Do what you want, as long as you're sure that's what you want.

PASHIK: I'm gonna go dance.

JENNY: The drum's calling.

JENNY kisses her goodbye and exits. PASHIK starts to warm up with a few more dance steps when NOBLE appears. PASHIK begins to dance and NOBLE slips up beside her and starts to dance, too, giving her a warm if nervous smile. PASHIK turns and walks away. NOBLE stops. PASHIK stops at a big rock and sits, her back to NOBLE. She picks up some rocks and throws them at a big trash bin, missing every time.

NOBLE: Hey.

PASHIK doesn't respond. She throws and misses again.

NOBLE: You got an arm like your father.

Still no answer.

NOBLE: I see. The silent treatment. Two can play at that game.

NOBLE sits down in front of her and proceeds to stare at her without saying a word. At first she tries to ignore him but his presence is too obvious. She turns, putting her back to him again.

NOBLE: Nice try, but I am fixing you with the Ojibway death stare. For your information, it is impossible to turn your back on the Ojibway death stare. At this very moment, it is eating through that pretty shawl on your back, and now through the cotton dress underneath it. Uh-oh, now I've reached the skin on your back. When's the last time you showered? Okay, now I take a left at the freckle and I slowly make my way through to the bone, then into the lungs and what do I see right before me? It's a teenager's heart. Oh my goodness gracious, if it isn't –

PASHIK: Cut it out.

NOBLE: She speaks. And what does she speak?

PASHIK: None of your business.

NOBLE: Not exactly a Shakespeare speech, but it's a beginning.

PASHIK: What do you want?

NOBLE: Various car parts and $40,800, but that seems unlikely. So right now I'll have to settle for a few words with you.

PASHIK: Don't put yourself out.

NOBLE: Hey, you think this is easy for me? Think again, kid. This isn't exactly my idea of fun either.

81

PASHIK: Then why are you here?

NOBLE: Why are any of us here? You're driving down a road going to someplace and you run low on gas or get a flat tire and you end up someplace else.

PASHIK: I'm a flat tire?!

NOBLE: I didn't mean it that way. I don't know how I meant it. I could use some help here.

PASHIK: Not from me.

NOBLE: Pashik! I didn't even know you existed. Honest. I'll even be more honest with you. Even if I knew about you, I don't know what would have happened. That was a long time ago. I was young, stupid ...

PASHIK: And desperate?

NOBLE: I guess. The point is, my only excuse is not knowing. If I were to blame you for everything you didn't know, where would we begin?

PASHIK: You should have known.

NOBLE: There's a lot of "shoulda's" in my life. That's only scratching the surface.

PASHIK: What about Mom?

NOBLE: What about her?

PASHIK: Are you, like, gonna get back with her?

NOBLE: Boy, the sun's hot today. Pashik, things don't work that way. I don't work that way. Life don't work that way.

PASHIK: I didn't think so. This isn't a movie, is it?

NOBLE: Nope. Graham Greene isn't here.

PASHIK: So you're my father.

NOBLE: Hold your applause.

PASHIK: You're nothing like I expected.

NOBLE: You're everything I didn't expect. Funny, huh? But I'm flattered you chose me to be your father.

PASHIK: Chose you? I don't get it.

NOBLE: I was once told that somewhere up there, before they're born, children choose their parents. In the great supermarket in the sky, as you were about to be born, you picked me on the shelf right beside the gourmet caviar, and your mother, right beside the nuts.

PASHIK: Do you believe that?

NOBLE: Beats the hell out of storks. You ever seen a stork? God, they're ugly birds.

PASHIK: That's a nice story.

NOBLE: The storks?

PASHIK: No. The thing about the babies choosing their parents.

NOBLE: That's why I never thought I'd have kids. Nobody would want me as a father. Who'da thought, huh? So, um, do you have any questions for me, of a sort of father-daughter kind?

PASHIK: Uh, yeah, does your family suffer from any sorts of hereditary insanity or diseases?

NOBLE: Just gas.

PASHIK: You're funny.

NOBLE: Funny looking? It runs in the family.

PASHIK: So, when are you leaving?

NOBLE: I'd like to as soon as possible. But I seem to be making your mom a bit on the skittish side and your mom's a dangerous woman when angry. And, unfortunately, you need an engine to move a car.

PASHIK: Oh, not again?! Mom does things like that. She's a great mechanic. Our basement is full of car parts and everything.

NOBLE: Good thing she's not a doctor.

The drumming starts up again.

NOBLE: I hear you dance. (*she nods*) Any good?

PASHIK: I've won some prizes.

NOBLE starts to dance, setting the pace. PASHIK watches for a moment then joins in. They dance, side by side, father and daughter. Pretty soon they become male/female mirrors of each other and they move in unity. They dance the length of the song, then stop, slightly winded, when the song ends.

NOBLE: You're good. Better than good. That came from me, you know.

PASHIK: You should see me when I have my whole outfit on.

NOBLE: Me, too.

PASHIK: When you leave, are you going to say goodbye to Mom?

NOBLE: If she let me, I would, but your mother wants me to be something I'm not. I'm willing to accept my way but she's not. So I'll just go on with my life and she'll go on with hers. And now that I've met you, I think she's got the better of the deal. And I still gotta figure some way of getting out of this *Twilight Zone* episode.

PASHIK: Maybe I can help. Stay right here.

Excited, PASHIK runs off. NOBLE watches her. It isn't long before SKUNK comes walking by, partially dressed in his dancing regalia. JENNY is with him. NOBLE zeros in on them.

JENNY: Really? Your car! Well, the raccoons around here will steal just about anything.

SKUNK: (*spotting NOBLE*) Hey, it's the man himself. Men's fancy dance competition in one hour. You ready?

NOBLE: Uh, Skunk, can I see you for a moment? Excuse us for a minute, Jenny.

SKUNK approaches NOBLE.

SKUNK: Sure. What's up? Wanna change the bet?

NOBLE grabs him by the shirt and speaks quietly.

NOBLE: Lay a finger on Pashik and I'll use your dick as a fan belt in my truck. Get the picture?

SKUNK: Got it.

NOBLE: (*releasing him*) Good. And as for the dance competition, I don't care who wins. It's yours, take it. Go do your thing and the best of luck to ya. I don't have five hundred dollars. And I don't even have fifty dollars but I don't care. I'm a thirty-eight-year-old man who has a great time doing what he's doing. I shouldn't have to justify it to you or anybody. Hopefully when you get to my age, you'll understand all this, but until then, you're a little mosquito in bright feathers. Enjoy it while you can because someday somebody will come and squash you. I was like you once, but hopefully I've grown out of it. Let's hope you do the same.

SKUNK: What's got into you?

85

NOBLE: I don't know and I don't care. Go off and play, and leave the thinking to us adults.

SKUNK: Ever crazy you ...

SKUNK exits. NOBLE approaches JENNY.

JENNY: What was all that about?

NOBLE: It's a guy thing.

JENNY: When isn't it? What did you do? Touch penises and bond?

NOBLE: Answer me one question. If I'm still the same guy I was all those years ago, do you really expect me to have $40,800 lying around to give you? Look at the way I'm dressed, for Christ's sake!

JENNY: I do realize it is highly unlikely.

NOBLE: Then what do you want from me? My truck, my liver, my soul! What?!

JENNY: All I want is for you to try. Not for me, for Pashik. She is seeing her father for the first time in her life. I don't want the only image she has of you to be your ponytail hightailing it out of the village. For her sake, I want to see you trying to be a man, to do something, to take care of things. I'm trying to show her someone she'll be proud of. And if I have to keep you on this reserve forever to do it, then for her sake I will.

NOBLE: Hey, I've got plenty to be proud of.

JENNY: The ability to undo a woman's bra with one hand while emptying a beer with the other is not something a seventeen-year-old girl can be proud of. She's a good kid. She deserves a decent father who's not afraid to look life in the eyes. The ironic thing is, you don't deserve a daughter like her.

NOBLE: This coming from a woman who steals car parts and relies on her hollow-tipped brothers to intimidate people?!

JENNY: Hey, a mother does what a mother has to.

NOBLE: No, a mother is love, not anger. She hugs, not threatens. I may not know a lot about this parenting thing, but I know that much. It didn't take a loaded gun to make me talk to Pashik. I did it on my own. And if you must know, I like her. And better still, I think she likes me. So you can keep your parental theories to yourself. I've got plenty to be proud of. And you, my dear, can go back to your basement full of car parts and be proud of that.

NOBLE storms away.

JENNY: (*to herself*) Not bad.

JENNY exits as NOBLE storms across the stage to AMOS's trailer where AMOS is filling the condiment bowls.

NOBLE: Hey, how's it going?

AMOS: You tell me.

NOBLE: I've got a daughter ...

AMOS: Does she have a father?

NOBLE: I'm working on it. Wiky wasn't built in a day, you know. But this is the best I've felt in a long time. But I do have one favour to ask. Can I bum a ride with you to the next powwow? Car's out of commission.

AMOS: I thought you gave it to Pashik.

NOBLE: Indirectly. So how about it? These cowboy boots weren't meant for walking.

AMOS: No problem. Actually, it'll give us a chance to talk. I'm getting kind of on in years, and this circuit is a killer for a man my age. I've been thinking about taking on a partner.

NOBLE: So?

AMOS: I'm talking about you, Noble.

NOBLE: Me? A partner? A Noble businessman. I don't know, Amos. The only business I know is giving people the business.

AMOS: Like everything else in this world, you learn with practice. Think it over. Still hit all the powwows with a little more security than before. Maybe pay off some old debts.

NOBLE: What are you, a Mohawk guardian angel?

Suddenly, PASHIK rushes in to NOBLE carrying a full plastic bag.

PASHIK: Here you are. Thought maybe you'd gone. Here, this is for you.

PASHIK hands the bag to NOBLE, who opens it and makes a discovery.

NOBLE: My carburetor and spark plugs. I'm free, my penance is over. But wait a minute, Fred and Howard are still watching the only road out of town.

PASHIK: Take the back road. When you get to the church, go straight instead of right. You'll see three big pine trees standing in a row. Turn on the dirt road right after them. That'll get you outside the village and onto the highway.

NOBLE: But don't Fred and Howard know about this road, too?

PASHIK: Yeah, but they don't know you know it. They'll just be watching the main road.

NOBLE: Thank you. Thank you a lot, but why are you doing this?

PASHIK: Mom shouldn't make you stay if you don't want to. It's not right.

NOBLE: Your mom says I owe her a lot of money.

PASHIK: Then pay her back when you can. I just want you to be happy.

NOBLE: Really?!

PASHIK: Uh-huh. And I went down into the basement with some friends and picked you out a nice set of whitewalls.

NOBLE: Whitewall tires!?

PASHIK: Nice shiny ones, too.

NOBLE: Shiny whitewall tires on a pickup. Oh boy.

PASHIK: We put them in the back of your truck. Well, I guess this is goodbye.

NOBLE: Pashik, are you proud of me?

PASHIK: Sure.

NOBLE: Why?

PASHIK: Because you're you.

NOBLE: Hey, do you still want to go to Connecticut next month? Just me and you? We'll be the best father-daughter team there.

PASHIK: Really! You mean it?

NOBLE: My offer is still open. I would really like to go with you.

PASHIK: But what about Mom, she'd never let me go. How would I get away?

NOBLE: Tell her you're going out to get some cigarettes and don't come back. Your mother's fallen for it before.

PASHIK: I don't think –

NOBLE: I'm kidding, just kidding. Don't worry, we'll work something out.

PASHIK throws her arms around NOBLE's neck and hugs. NOBLE hugs her back.

PASHIK: I can't believe it.

NOBLE: We're going to Connecticut.

PASHIK: You're so wonderful.

NOBLE: So are you. Maybe you can teach me some new steps.

PASHIK: And you can teach me some old ones.

NOBLE: I'd love to. You better go get ready, grand entry is in a few minutes.

PASHIK: Okay. Bye ... Dad.

NOBLE: Bye.

PASHIK exits and AMOS approaches.

NOBLE: That's my daughter.

AMOS: So I heard. How did that word "Dad" feel?

NOBLE: I'm still on my feet this time.

AMOS: Nothing quite like it, is there?

NOBLE: Nope.

AMOS: I thought I heard the word "Connecticut" mentioned. You taking her?

NOBLE: Yep. Try and stop me. Especially since I can now fix my car and get out of here. Have you seen Summer?

AMOS: Actually I have. That's the other thing I wanted to talk to you about.

SUMMER comes out of the trailer with some fortune scones.

SUMMER: Oh, hi Noble. (*to AMOS*) Have you told him?

AMOS: I was just getting to that. Um, Noble, there have been some developments.

NOBLE: What developments?

AMOS slips his arm around SUMMER and she does the same.

NOBLE: You're kidding!

SUMMER: Are you angry? I mean, it just looked to me like you were having some personal problems and I didn't want to add to them 'cause, Creator knows, our people have enough problems as it is without me adding to them. So I came to Amos for advice and we got to talking and well ...

AMOS: I love being an elder.

SUMMER: And Amos has promised to teach me everything about my aboriginal heritage this summer. I will be so prepared for school it will be ridiculous. I knew going to powwows would change my life. Isn't he wonderful?

NOBLE: Yeah, I could just hug him to death.

AMOS: Summer, could you make sure we have enough pop for the weekend? There'll be a lot of thirsty people under this sun.

91

SUMMER: Sure thing. I wonder if I can get a business credit for this too?

SUMMER exits.

NOBLE: So you get the girl and I get a job.

AMOS: I think you need a job more than you need her.

NOBLE: It's amazing how far you can get being one-sixty-fourth.

AMOS: It's always been my belief that if there's one drop of Native blood in her, she's my daughter. And I will honour that.

NOBLE: Under the circumstances, I'd reword that "daughter" part, if you know what I mean.

AMOS: Good point.

NOBLE: Well, always the bridesmaid, never the bride. I might as well go put my car together. It's time to hear "On the Road Again."

AMOS: Need help? I got tools in the trunk.

NOBLE: Sure. Say there, Amos, I don't suppose you'd be interested in a set of brand-spanking-new shiny whitewall tires?

AMOS: Do I look that senile? No, thank you. How the hell did you get whitewall tires?

NOBLE: Pashik gave them to me.

AMOS: Then you should keep them. I mean, it's your daughter's first gift to you, her father. It's a bad start if you sell or give them away.

NOBLE: Oh, wonderful. I'll be buried with a set of whitewall tires. At least I'll be going to heaven in style.

NOBLE starts taking his watch and rings off, rolls up his sleeves, and begins to take his choker off in front of AMOS.

NOBLE: Well, let's go attack that beast. You work on the plugs, I'll tackle the carburetor.

AMOS: I've been admiring that choker of yours. Nice piece of workmanship.

NOBLE: Thanks. Yeah, I've had it for years. My mom made it for me. They're a common design up where I come from.

AMOS: I know. I've been up there. In fact, I used to know a beautiful Ojibway woman up that way, made me one just like it back when I worked up near Sudbury.

NOBLE: Wonder who she was?

AMOS: Boy, that must have been back, oh, in the mid-fifties I'd say. I sure fancied that lady. Was almost gonna marry her. I often wonder what happened to Margaret Blackfish.

NOBLE turns around with a big, wide-eyed expression on his face. He peers closely into AMOS's eyes.

NOBLE: Dad?!

NOBLE passes out again, soon followed by AMOS.

The lights go down.

THE END

The Baby Blues

Lyrics: Drew Hayden Taylor
Music: Lorne Cardinal
David DeLeary

Harmonica improvises on a blues scale

1: I
2: The
3: Let's

got in my truck and drove all the way here, Ho-ping to find some-one to
nights are long and the days are hot. The beer may be cold but ba-by I'm not
put our lips to-ge - ther and ba-by we'll hum To - ge-ther we'll be loud - er

1. call my sweet dear.

3. than the big-gest drum.

The road was dus-ty and the jour-ney long, Ho-ping for some fun, am I
I've got a fire for two and a kiss for one, Come on ho-ney, I can
Per - son to per-son and Na - tion to Na- tion, Be - fore we're done,

right or am I wrong? I've got the Ba - by Blues,
be a lot of fun.
they'll call the Fire Sta - tion.

you got it too. Look-ing for love, ev' - ry place I go.

When it comes to snag-gin', I'm a pro I've got the

Ba - by Blues right down to my toes I'm a hope-less ro-man-tic with

Harmonica fill

no - thing to lose.

Note: The harmonica is free to interject at any time in the phrasing. This is suposed to be a very loose, spontaneous performance.